D0148482

Piedmont
College Library
Demorest, Ga.
83266
Class 378.198 Book C66

Freshman Seminar

Other Titles in This Series

Teaching Strategies for the College Classroom, James R. Davis

A Handbook on Open Admissions, Anne F. Decker, Ruth Jody, and Felicia Brings

A College in Dispersion: Women at Bryn Mawr, 1896-1975, edited by Ann F. Miller

Planning for Higher Education: Background and Applications, Allan O. Pfnister

Westview Special Studies in Higher Education

Freshman Seminar: A New Orientation
Robert D. Cohen and Ruth Jody

The competition for students is growing among colleges and universities, leading administrators and student personnel professionals to ask what they can do to recruit and retain their students without lowering academic standards. The Freshman Seminar is one answer: it is a full-semester course designed to train would-be students in the skills they will need to survive in a student's world. Remedial courses alone are not sufficient; there are a host of meta-academic activities to be mastered, among them note taking, test taking, class participation, interacting with instructors, and developing realistic attitudes towards learning.

The authors, initiators and experienced teachers in Hunter College's Freshman Seminar Program, describe the rationale for such a course, as well as its value. Their step-by-step approach to establishing and teaching a freshman seminar details the fundamentals of curriculum design and teaching methods and describes specific instructional material for classroom use—lesson plans, games, attitude inventories, and role playing.

This is a comprehensive and practical guidebook for the college administrator who wants to reduce student attrition and for the student personnel professional who will implement such a program.

Robert D. Cohen is assistant to the dean of students at Hunter College, where he has coordinated the Freshman Seminar Program since its inception in 1972. He holds an Ed.D. in higher education from Teachers College, Columbia University.

Ruth Jody, director of tutorial services at Hunter College, is coauthor of *A Handbook on Open Admissions* (Westview Press, 1976).

Freshman Seminar: A New Orientation

Robert D. Cohen and Ruth Jody

Westview Press/ Boulder, Colorado

Westview Special Studies in Higher Education

Published in 1978 in the United States of America by
Westview Press, Inc.
5500 Central Avenue
Boulder, Colorado 80301
Frederick A. Praeger, Publisher

Library of Congress Cataloging in Publication Data
Cohen, Robert Douglas, 1938-
Freshman seminar.
(Westview special studies in higher education)
Bibliography: p.
1. College student orientation. I. Jody, Ruth. joint author. II. Title.
LB2343.3.C63 378.1'98 78-1682
ISBN 0-89158-098-0
ISBN 0-89158-099-9 pbk.

Printed and bound in the United States of America

Contents

1

The Need for Ongoing Orientation

Orientation of new students to college has for many years in most colleges taken the form of massive get-togethers either during the period just before classes begin or during the summer preceding the freshman year. It has been seen as a time for students to meet other students, take tours of the college, and hear college faculty and administrators talk about the college. These programs, socially satisfying as they might be, have not addressed themselves at any length and in any depth to new students' needs to learn about the college system and how to deal with it. Indeed, until recently, given a college-prepared population, the institution could safely assume that its freshmen were arriving equipped to adapt on their own; the peer culture, with its formal and informal groups, would take care of the socialization process and further provide various settings for learning about the college system. Moreover, institutionalized schemes for helping students' adaptation to college might be viewed as a throwback to the earlier years of *in loco parentis;* this was highly unpopular, both among students and educators in the 1960s.

But a number of factors came together in the later 1960s and the 1970s to make the brief pre-college orientation programs less than desirable. First, admissions criteria in many public colleges and universities were drastically changed; students who hadn't expected to go to college and therefore hadn't been trained in the skills of studenthood were now facing the very different demands of college. Second, and related to this, the colleges' internal systems, in response to dealing with their new populations, became themselves more complex; new remedial sequences of courses were added, new regulations devised, complicating the choices students had to make. And third, the peer culture and its various agencies, once so success-oriented, seemed, by the 1970s, to have lost much of their potency in helping students to adapt.

All of these factors alerted educators to the need for some new way to provide an ongoing setting for students to make a successful transition to the college environment. This book deals with the ongoing orientation program as a method for helping students to make this transition. We conceive of three components to effect this adaptation to college life: (1) an attitudinal shift from passivity to assertiveness with regard to the educational system; (2) the possession of information about the resources of the institution and about the possibilities in the post-college world, and (3) the competence in the scholastic skills necessary for success in academic courses.

Shift from Passivity

The ultimate goal of Freshman Seminar is an attitudinal one: to help the entering college student to view himself as an active participant in the process of learning, and not as a passive recipient of an educational system.

Moving toward this goal depends upon the slow and steady unlearning of previously learned attitudes. In his high school years, the student's success was likely to have come from his obedience to the system as much as from his competence in learning. In urban settings especially, the student who causes no trouble is passed on from grade to grade with but meager regard for how much or how well he has learned. What such a student *has* learned—that attendance and obedience are rewarded—is inapplicable in the college setting. It is therefore not surprising that a college that rewards intellectual competence and offers the student so much freedom of movement and choice turns the new student's world topsy-turvy. There are no hall monitors patrolling the corridors, no truant officers tracking down truants, no study halls, no forced lunch periods. Students first experiencing this absence of coercive authority may conclude that the college has no rules and regulations whatsovever. Or they may suspect that what rules there are are elusive and unstated; if they find out what they are, they may have to observe them. The truth about the authority of the college is that it is likely to be different and more complex than the kinds of authority the entering student has previously learned to live with. Getting students to recognize the nature of college authority and deal with it is one of the major aims of Freshman Seminar.

No statutes require people to go or to stay in college. The forces that motivate students' attendance are social and economic; these may be profound and inescapable indeed, but they are much more implicit than are truant officers. Most students need help in making explicit to themselves the sources of their motivation to attend college. And once they are attending, they find they must also seek out the rules and regulations, the institution's terms, under which they make their way as students. Since the high school's requirements were most likely to have been mapped out and enforced most explicitly by the authorities, the college student is going to need a new stock of attitudinal tools with which to make choices and take action by himself.

Quite predictably, merely stating the necessity for self-initiative will not take the students very far in changing attitudes. It is in *training* for self-initiative that the Seminar does its work. It takes patience, prodding, and probing on the part of a skilled instructor. It takes time and some experience of the college's demands for the student to recognize that there is even a need for relearning. The student naturally expects that the passivity that worked so well for so long will also work for him at the college.

Possession of Information

Although the increasing proliferation of course and career choices may be more problematic for the academically unprepared, it is hardly limited to this group. A good science student, for example, faces many areas of study that were rarely offered twenty-five years ago and must choose before moving into graduate study. In psychology, an undergraduate major looking for advanced programs encounters a bewildering array of supposedly specialized areas: social psychology, school psychology, clinical psychology, etc. With rare exceptions, the high schools offer the same subjects today as they did twenty or thirty years ago. The gap between what most high school graduates are familiar with and what colleges offer is wide indeed.

Let us recount an instructor's experience in Hunter's Freshman Seminar. He was helping students prepare their course choices for the following semester. Students had their trusty catalogs in front of them. "What's the difference between this cultural anthropology and the physical anthropology?" one student asked. The instructor explained the difference, to which one student responded, "So cultural anthropology sounds like sociology and physical anthropology is the same as archaeology?" The pained instructor, now suspecting he had assumed too much, asked the class what, for him, was an embarrassing question, "How many of you have heard the words *anthropology* or *sociology* before this class session, or before you read the catalog? Honestly now." Two hands shot up for each word, the same students for each. One who'd heard of sociology said it was the study of "welfare programs and juvenile delinquency."

If this anecdote sounds familiar, and could occur in colleges throughout the United States, it tells us of a crying need. Entering college students need someone knowledgeable and trustworthy who can help them decipher and process the information they require to make intelligent choices. The Freshman Seminar instructor's goal is to do just that in a structured group setting. This will be referred to later in the book.

Competence in Scholastic Skills

In addition to their need for information, entering students need training in the skills of studenthood, training above and beyond the kinds of basic academic skills provided by remedial courses. At the City University of New York, when the open admissions policy was begun in 1970, the constituent senior colleges responded quickly enough to the anticipated need for pre-college level courses in math and English. But it took them somewhat longer to understand that what they had considered "remediation" needed an expanded definition and program. Basic math and English were of course necessary. But a whole range of what we might call "scholastic" skills was lacking in these new students. By "scholastic" skills we mean, broadly, those attitudes and behaviors necessary for enacting successfully the role of student in and out of the classroom.

What are some of these areas of behavior? Taking notes in a lecture is one of them. Most entering college students, academically prepared or not, have not experienced the lecture hall setting as a learning environment. Those who are brave enough to betray their bewilderment will come up to lecturers after class and and ask them what they should be getting down in their notes. Or advisors will hear their complaints: "That guy just talks and talks; there's no time to understand what he's talking *about.*" Whether the lecture method is pedagogically desirable is irrelevant; it is a fact of college life. Clearly, entering students have not learned, let alone practiced, what most psychologists call "attending behavior" for extended periods of time. Their bewilderment is therefore not surprising. What is surprising is that educators had assumed that students possessed these skills. Listening skills have rarely been taught at the college level; remedial English courses generally concentrated on reading and writing, and lecturers in the various academic departments were not about to take lecture time to teach note-taking. An essential skill for college learners, heretofore taken for granted, was ignored.

Note-taking is but one of many necessary scholastic skills. In the classroom, students need to know how to participate productively, ask questions of instructors, and take examinations. Out-of-class skills include study skills, time management, and decision making, the last of which for the college student involves course choice, selection of major and minor, and career choice. If we add to the teaching of these skills the presentation of information about college regulations and organization, it will be seen that the curriculum of a Freshman Seminar goes well beyond the one-day or one-week pre-college orientation program. Moreover, Freshman Seminar curriculum demands, unlike the one-shot orientation, a setting in which students can *practice* using information and skills. That means a program run over a period of time, for students need time to practice skills as well as time for the absorption of information and timely opportunities to use it.

What Does Freshman Seminar Offer the College?

Once a college or university determines that students need to learn the skills and behaviors we have outlined, it remains for the institution to assess its own interest in meeting that need. Each college has limited financial and educational resources. If, for example, students need recreational activity, the college doesn't automatically allocate its funds toward building pools and tennis courts, particularly if these facilities are available elsewhere in the local community. A Freshman Seminar venture must similarly be assessed in terms of the college's overall educational mission and priorities.

If the college is in the privileged position of having a college-prepared clientele, with many more applicants than can be accepted, then of course Freshman Seminar may not be a priority. What problems arise in students' adaptation to college can be handled on a case-by-case basis. Further, such a college can, without fear of losing tuition income, take a sink-or-swim attitude toward students academically.

But fewer higher education institutions are finding themselves in such a position. With the college-age cohorts shrinking in the 1970s, colleges have been forced to search for new clientele: senior citizens, women who had deferred college for marriage and motherhood, workers seeking education as a means of changing careers. If these colleges are to maintain their educational standards, and yet admit the marginally prepared student, the new clientele will require some training in the skills of studenthood. Otherwise, the new entrants may be dropped out in a semester or two. Some attrition in the freshman year is of course to be expected. Students drop out for many nonacademic reasons that the college cannot forestall. But students' bewilderment in the face of college demands is not one of these. A planned, focused program such as Freshman Seminar gives the college a chance to keep students enrolled who might otherwise abandon their college education because they are ignorant of or confused about what college studenthood requires.

A solid orientation to college regulations and resources has other practical dividends for the college as well. It fosters the appropriate use of helping services, which in many colleges are underutilized because students are unfamiliar with what these services offer. It fosters the reduction of "trial-and-error" behavior by students who miss deadlines, who take courses over their heads, and who ask the wrong questions in the wrong places. In short, extended orientation can reduce the consumption of administrative time by educating the consumer—the student—in how to use the resources of the college.

Summary

The traditional freshman orientation, which has consisted of a day's or week's introduction to the college, is inadequate for helping students to learn about the college system and how to deal with it. Recent changes in many colleges' admission criteria, and subsequent changes in their internal organization, have given rise to the need for an extended orientation effort that continues for an entire semester.

New student populations need help in viewing themselves as active participants in the learning process. They need help in acquiring information about the rules and resources of a college. And they need training in the various skills of studenthood such as note-taking, test-taking, and participation in class discussions. The Freshman Seminar focuses on offering such help in these three areas.

The college that needs to maintain its enrollment without lowering academic standards has much to gain by offering a Freshman Seminar program. As noted, it can keep students enrolled who might otherwise drop out. Seminar fosters students' appropriate use of helping services, the reduction of trial-and-error behavior by students who miss the deadlines or who take inappropriate courses. By educating the student to understand the demands of the college environment, Freshman Seminar can reduce the expenditure of costly administrative time.

Students' needs to understand their new environment and their role in it can no longer be left to chance. A programmatic effort by the institution in this direction not only benefits students but also serves the institution's needs to keep its students.

2
Planning for a Freshman Seminar Program

How does a college go about setting up a Freshman Seminar Program? What issues must be decided before a prospectus is presented to the authority within the institution that must give its approval?

The Initial Planning

Ideally, the initial planning should be done by a group that has a broad base within the college. Without the support of the administrative chief of student services, the dean of students, or vice-president for student affairs, chances for successfully launching a Seminar program are greatly reduced from the start. A green light from the dean or vice-president should be considered a necessity even before the initial planning committee is chosen, and a brief appearance by the dean at the first meeting is a wise move.

The planning committee should include people such as faculty advisors who have had firsthand experience with students for whom the Seminar would be helpful. Faculty advisors are the ones most likely to bridge the gap between student service staff and the "teaching-only" faculty. If the college is organized into divisions (humanities, social sciences, etc.), it would be wise to enlist the efforts of one person from each division. Together with the initiators of the Seminar from student services, this group of six to eight can put together the first Seminar proposal.

An alternative to the broad-based committee is a group from within the service areas themselves. At Hunter College, this is in fact how we launched the original proposal. Two separate and somewhat competing service offices drew up plans, got together to hammer out a single proposal, and presented that proposal to the Hunter College Senate. Teaching faculty had not been consulted during the initial planning, and no one outside the service area was prepared to speak for the proposal at the Senate meeting. The resistance our proposal raised at this public forum seemed as much the result of leaving the faculty out of the planning as it was of opposition to the educational validity of the Seminar itself. This tactical error in planning put us on the defensive. Despite the fact that our proposal was approved, its totally service-based sponsorship was perceived by many other faculty as limiting its credibility. Sponsorship, therefore, from a coalition of groups within the college seems more desirable in getting the Seminar off to a good start.

Should Seminar Be a Course?

The most rudimentary issue to be decided is whether Freshman Seminar should take the form of a course or an extracurricular activity for entering students. If it is offered as an extracurricular activity, as a series of small-group meetings or workshops, then many of the problems of a Seminar course are avoided: you needn't be concerned with the thorny question of academic credit, of grading, of course requirements. And you are likely to get only the most motivated students to take part in the Seminar program, a decidedly pleasurable situation for any teacher. The number of participants is likely to be low, yet success with already motivated students is likely to be high. If Seminar is offered in this format, publicizing it through departmental advisors, posters, brochures, and ads in the college news media becomes an absolute necessity.

But offering Freshman Seminar as a voluntary, no matter how highly recommended, extracurricular activity has a major drawback. Students tend to regard any out-of-class activity as of secondary importance, or, if important, important as fun, not work. Granted, college athletes often work and slave at their sport, but their potential rewards in fame and fortune are an institutionalized part of the American Dream. Working at the skills of studenthood is hardly an attractive after-school sport for most students, and those students who find it so are probably well on their way to successful studenthood anyhow.

If it is decided that Freshman Seminar will be a course, the number of further decisions grows appreciably. The planning committee will have to confront the issues of credit, grading, and appropriate staffing.

The Question of Credit

Academic credit is usually attached to the successful completion of a course. Whether Freshman Seminar should be a course for credit becomes an issue because its content is outside the traditional bounds of academic subjects. Seen as *preparation for* studenthood rather than the actual exercise of skill and competency, Freshman Seminar will be regarded by some as not deserving of college credit. And yet if the college gives academic credit for the learning of such skills as essay writing in freshman composition, why should it not give credit for the learning of, say, note-taking skills?

There is a clearly pragmatic argument for credit as well. A course is not likely to be regarded as a course unless it carries with it a credit payoff for students. Furthermore, the importance of the skills Freshman Seminar teaches will be enhanced only if the course bears the "coin" of the academic realm, which is credit toward the degree.

The planning committee's decision with regard to credit has to take into account the educational stance of the particular college. If the very notion of a Freshman Seminar course would seem a radical idea for a college, then asking for the course to be credited might doom its acceptance before the college's governing body. If, on the other hand, remedial and other pre–college level courses are being offered with credit, then credit for Seminar should not be such a radical departure, particularly if only one credit is requested for one hour's class per week.

The experience of the colleges of the City University of New York suggests that noncredit courses falter and disappear and that credit courses are taken seriously by both faculty and students. At Hunter, where students taking remedial courses were required to take Freshman Seminar, the awarding of credit eased student resentment and forced the staff to make the content worthy of the credit given. After several semesters of offering Seminar, students not required to take the course heard about it and opted for it, in numbers so great that staff could not be found to handle all the sections. In other words, the credit factor seemed to increase the number of students voluntarily enrolling in the course.

Grading Seminar

Where the option exists to depart from the traditional grading system with "pass/fail" or "credit/no credit," it is tempting to use this alternate system for Freshman Seminar. The University of South Carolina's University 101 offers three ungraded credits for its course, and Hunter College's Freshman Seminar awards one graded credit. The non-graded approach has perhaps the advantages of reducing students' anxieties and taking away the struggle for a grade, which can be detrimental to the student-teacher relationship. On the other hand, however, if there is indeed content and material to be learned in Seminar, the degree to which this material is learned is appropriately represented by a grade. A less obvious advantage of using grading in Seminar is that the reality of grading, of being judged, is brought home to students in a setting in which they *are* graded; both students and instructors can avoid this reality when grades are eliminated.

A third option on the grading issue would leave the choice of grading system to the individual student. In colleges where the student rather than the instructor makes such a decision, this may be the wisest policy for Freshman Seminar. For it allows in Seminar the same options that are available to students in many other courses as well. If Seminar is too different structurally from other courses at the college, it cannot be used as a model of what students have generally to deal with in other courses.

Staffing Freshman Seminar

Choosing an instructional staff for Seminar is ultimately going to boil down to the practical question of who is interested and available. But it is nonetheless essential for the Seminar planners first to consider the overall staffing possibilities. Would teaching faculty be better at teaching Seminar than full-time counselors and advisors? Or vice versa? Should junior and senior students take a role in teaching Seminar? These are questions that must be discussed. In the following segment of this chapter, we will focus on the staffing potential of four groups: faculty; student personnel staff, including counselors; undergraduate students; and graduate students.

Faculty

Every college in which faculty members take on out-of-classroom tasks is made aware of the struggles and rewards of doing so. The closer such tasks are tied to the primary educational work of the faculty member, the more likely he is to want to do it and do it well. Advising prospective and already declared majors has clearly been the job of faculty in each academic department. For some, it is a burden; for others, a pleasure. The same holds for teaching Freshman Seminar. For although Seminar instruction *is* a teaching task, the content is, for most faculty people, rather far afield from their main professional interests. Still, particularly in the behavioral sciences, there may be a number of willing and skilled teachers who will be eager to try this fresh venture in teaching.

The first principle in selecting staff is to let them select themselves. To make this possible, of course, they must first know what the job entails. The course description should be reasonably detailed and yet open-ended with regard to teaching methods and styles. A course description such as the one in Appendix A should be widely distributed throughout the college, together with a cover letter inviting those interested in teaching to attend a meeting. In addition, department chairpersons and faculty advisors should be contacted by members of the planning committee and asked to recommend likely candidates.

Even if recruitment of Seminar staff from faculty ranks does not work out, for budgetary and other reasons, it is important that they receive a course description and an invitation to participate. For then the Seminar idea will have had wide dissemination throughout the college before it is up for approval as a course. The Seminar is less likely to be perceived as some mysterious or frivolous scheme of the college shrinks or as an attempt at empire building, but as a rational, serious, and structured plan for helping students to be competent in the skills of studenthood.

Teaching Seminar is only one way in which faculty can participate in it. Faculty members can and should be asked to make guest appearances at Seminar sessions, where their expertise in a particular area may be far greater than that of the instructor himself. There may be, for example, a psychology professor who could talk with students about test anxiety. Or a historian who would be eager to discuss with Seminar students the history of higher education, or the history of their own college. Again, faculty participation of this kind not only enriches the Seminar classroom; it serves to attune broader segments of the college community to what Seminar is and does.

Counselors and Other Student Personnel Professionals

Whatever the extent of faculty teaching of Seminar, the core group of teaching staff may well come from the ranks of nonteaching professionals, those counselors and other student personnel workers who have been trained to work with students who have academic and personal problems. But even this group may think that teaching Seminar is not entirely in concert with their interests and training. Let us consider the issue of a counseling center's reluctance to take on Seminar teaching and suggest some reasons why teaching Seminar may indeed be in their professional interest.

As a *support* service, the college counseling center is, in times of budgetary stress, viewed by college administrators as more expendable than direct instructional services. In recent years, student support services have been called upon to justify their share of the college budget, which they can best do by engaging in work that is central to the welfare of substantial numbers of students.

If the results of a 1973 survey of college counseling centers are any indication, there is little movement in this direction. Lombardi found that an average of only 6.5 per cent of counseling time was spent on counseling students about difficulties with academic work; the largest category of staff time was spent in "short-term counseling on personal problems."[1] What exactly "short-term" means in terms of length or frequency of counseling sessions is not defined, nor does the survey present any figures on what percentage of college populations the counselors saw. But it would seem that counseling centers are spending much of their resources on relatively intensive work with relatively few students.

Leaving aside the question of how appropriate it is for intensive personal counseling to be offered in the college setting, there is good reason why preventive outreach activity such as Freshman Seminar is appropriate and, furthermore, justifiable in terms of the college budget.

There is general agreement among support service personnel that the transition from high school to college requires much adaptation on the part of the student and that the increasing competitiveness of college faces students with stresses not previously experienced. Why then do counseling centers continue to wait for students' crises before they do their work? Why can't counseling services engage students in preventive training to help students anticipate the stresses of college life?

The reluctance of counseling personnel to do preventive outreach may derive from assumptions learned in traditional psychotherapeutic training: (1) that the client/patient must *initiate* the search for help; (2) that help-seeking behavior is motivated by one's experience of emotional pain; and (3) that the outcome of therapy is personality change. Even through counseling, insofar as it is different from psychotherapy, aims "to facilitate development" rather than to change personality, the Freudian model still seems to hold sway among those trained as counselors.[2] It is not surprising, therefore, that the counselor, regardless of the setting he works in, will place a higher professional value on doing personal, in-depth treatment. Outreach activity, particularly in the unaccustomed setting of a classroom, is likely to be regarded as of low professional value. If counselors are to teach Freshman Seminar, they must be persuaded that this setting indeed provides them an opportunity to be agents of personal change, even if the material presented by their students seems not as dramatic or agonizing as that presented by student clients who seek individual help. In the Seminar class, suggestions for changes in study behaviors, say, can have a slow, steady effect on students' concepts of themselves as competent learners. What the counselor/instructor does to facilitate change will be seen in the following example.

A student who consistently froze on exams and whose study behavior was highly ritualized was encouraged by the Seminar instructor and by other students in the class *not* to study on the day of the examination, "just to see how it worked." "I wouldn't risk it in my next exam, not in *that* course," said the student. "How about a course you're doing well in already," the instructor suggested. "Okay, I'll try it in economics." He did, and was astounded by his lack of anxiety and the ease with which he wrote his exam paper. After reporting the good news back to the class, others tried the same approach; with some it worked, with others it didn't. But it enabled the first student to "try out" other changes in studying, until he was no longer stuck with a set of unproductive rituals he had previously regarded as immutable.

The point here is that the counselor as Seminar instructor can indeed facilitate change. And just because he is not in his office or because he does not need to bring all of his analytical wisdom to a problem does not mean that he is any less effective an agent of change than he is in the clinical setting.

One final reason why counseling service people should teach Seminar is that personal counseling cases are likely to arise out of the counselor/student relationships that build throughout the semester of classroom contact. Access to the counselor as a one-to-one helping agent, in other words, is opened up to the student through his contact with the counselor as a classroom instructor.

Students as Seminar Instructors

The pre-semester format of freshman orientation has in most cases depended largely upon the voluntary or paid participation of upperclassmen. For a massive, intensive pre-college orientation program, this makes sense. The rationale for using peers for continuing orientation programs such as Freshman Seminar, however, requires some qualification. It is argued that peer-led programs are less expensive, that they provide learning opportunities for the students who run them, and that peers can more readily communicate with freshmen than can a professional staff.

If students are used either as instructors or as assistants in Freshman Seminar, they must be recruited, trained, and supervised. This in itself requires professional staff time and, therefore, expense. Another expense is remuneration for the upperclassmen, either academic credit or direct pay, both of which cost the college. It is a moot point whether student staffing of ongoing orientation produces a savings.

Granted, teaching or assisting in the teaching of Seminar can be valuable experience for the upperclassmen and for the Seminar students. After all, the upperclassman has survived the first few years of college and can be seen by freshmen as a model and a resource. But freshmen tend to lionize the authority of an upperclassman, who at the same time is—all too often—not so securely self-identified that he can shed the all-knowing role placed upon him. His acceptance of this role can therefore be at the expense of the freshmen who look to him as the fount of knowledge.

But freshmen have many other opportunities to learn from older peers. If the peer culture is indeed the major agent of college student adaptation, it does not follow that its primacy is desirable. For dependence upon the peer group as authority tends to perpetuate the antagonism between the late adolescent and the adult community, thus sustaining his sense that adults are the enemy and that peers are the allies of the incoming student. Although it is possible to use a helpful peer in Freshman Seminar, it is yet more important that an adult, the instructor, be the major helping agent in the program. Only in this way can a student begin to break through the notion that adults per se are the opposing force. Repeatedly, college students have reported that their breakthrough to viewing *themselves* as adults has been fostered by a meaningful relationship with an adult: a professor, a counselor, a friend of the family.[3] A continuing orientation program that relies solely on older students as staff robs freshmen of at least one opportunity to develop this kind of relationship with an adult. Even having upperclassmen as assistants may attenuate the possibilities for the development of such a relationship in the classroom; if a freshman can choose whether to relate to a peer or to an adult, he will often choose the peer, since that is an emotionally easier choice.

Surely, freshmen need to relate to peers. In Seminar sessions where upperclassmen come in as guest participants, there often seems to be instant rapport and high satisfaction. But it would be shortsighted to use this as a rationale for reducing the professional staff leadership in the program. Struggles between Seminar students and the instructor are inevitable and, temporarily, uncomfortable; fewer such struggles may seem to occur when students are relating to an upperclassman. But the sparring with adult authority in the Seminar is necessary; unless a setting is provided in which it can happen, be discussed, and resolved, the student may remain silently warring with adult authority throughout his college career and beyond it.

Graduate Students

If professional staff resources are too limited to allow their full staffing of Seminar, an alternative is to use graduate student interns from one of the helping professions: counseling, student personnel, or social work. These students' teaching of Seminar can become a full-fledged field experience, with ample time for training and supervision. They are likely to view it as a serious step in their training for professional careers. Further, as people who have chosen a helping profession and are actively training for it, they will probably be more equipped than are undergraduates to deal with problems of authority that students bring into the Seminar classroom. They will be at least four years older than most of their students and hence will be perceived as adults by their students.

The biggest disadvantage of staffing with graduate students is their unfamiliarity with the college itself, unless of course they are recent graduates of the same institution. This can be corrected by training sessions, to be sure, but graduate students do have to catch up with the purely informational component of the Seminar curriculum.

Assigning Students to Seminar Sections: Homogeneity vs. Heterogeneity

On what basis should students be assigned to particular Seminar sections? This is not an issue that need be settled for inclusion in the course description, but it would be wise for the planning committee to discuss it well before students register for Seminar, for it has educational implications.

If it were possible to have, say, a nursing students' Seminar group or an engineering students' section, would this not allow a clearer curricular focus in each such group? Perhaps, although there is a corresponding disadvantage: freshmen in Seminar sections of their own discipline may miss the stimulation of those in other disciplines and are probably less likely to consider examining their career direction if kept in a homogeneous group.

There is some indication that students themselves have no preference between a homogeneous or heterogeneous group. John Gardner, director of the University of South Carolina's University 101 Program reports that:

> we have found that the typical USC freshman has no interest at all in taking a University 101 class taught by an instructor of a particular discipline. Their primary concern is to simply get the course and to get it at a time of day that is convenient for them. In fact, for two semesters consecutively I tried publishing and disseminating a masterfully done biographical statement on each participating faculty member. These statements were provided to freshmen at registration so that they could select the course by

professor. There was no interest in this at all and proved to be a vast waste of clerical time and resources.[4]

Ironically, it is *through* the Seminar that we hope to help freshmen choose courses and sections for reasons other than time convenience. Perhaps it is too much to expect an entering freshman to use more learning-centered criteria. In any case, if we can generalize at all about the South Carolina experience, we can guess that students will not use the option to select a Seminar section on the basis of career or major interest.

The Seminar planners could, however, decide to *place* students in sections appropriate to their major, taught by an instructor from their discipline, and geared to their particular academic interest. Since students in highly structured programs such as nursing or engineering often have little or no choice of courses, one could assign such students to sections they *do* have a time slot for. But what would be the educational advantage of forcing such groupings?

The instructor could make some generally safe assumptions about his students' common interest in his field. He could present material about the field, check students' perceptions about the careers they are training for, help them explore their motivation for the particular work, and discuss the attitudes, values, and learning skills necessary for that work. Nurses, for example, could deal with the problems of taking orders in the rigid hospital hierarchy; they could discuss and compare values about maintaining life regardless of the patient's condition. These are issues that may be more productively discussed in a homogeneous group of nursing students than in a mixed Seminar section.

What would be missing in a homogeneous group are students from outside the particular discipline upon which the grouping is based. We must ask, then, why should we expose our nursing students to other students in Seminar.

Don't nursing students need all the peer and faculty support they can get to adapt to their rigorous training? Indeed they do, and they get it aplenty in their nursing classes and from their peer culture. The problem is that for freshmen who have already chosen a career direction, the forces are quite strong for their sustaining that interest. What these students lack is a setting in which they can raise and voice doubts about their career choice, which may be premature. The presence of students in Seminar who have either made *other* choices or are still undecided can provide both a challenge and an opportunity to the career-fixed student.

Despite the particular advantages and disadvantages of a homogeneous group based on common career or major interest, we must not lose sight of the more general interests *all* freshmen share. Obviously, they are all students, and all are new to the particular college. They share the tasks of adapting to their new environment, of understanding and meeting its demands. In other words, even the most randomly assigned collection of Seminar students can become a group. If we were to assign students by career interest, they would have of course a special focus for their "groupness." Whether that special focus is necessary or desirable is another question. For some of these reasons, then, we may want to keep Seminar sections less rather than more homogeneous; students' similarity as students and as freshmen offers us enough basis on which to develop an interacting group.

The planning committee, after considering all the pros and cons, may still want to try a few homogeneous groupings along with a few randomly assigned sections. In so doing, they will give the Seminar coordinator a chance to assess the contentions we have made: that a heterogeneous section tends to yield richer discussions and that a homogeneous section tends to reinforce the homogeneity that its students bring to it.

Summary

After getting the backing of the administrative head of support services, the initiators of Freshman Seminar should put together a planning committee that includes a broad base of faculty members. This committee will discuss and settle a number of issues before writing a course description for presentation to the body that must approve the program.

The first decision facing the planners is whether Seminar is to be offered as a course or as an extracurricular activity. A major drawback of Seminar as an extracurricular activity is that it reduces its importance in the eyes of the students. If Seminar is offered as a course, many other decisions must be made: credit vs. no credit, and, if credit, graded vs. nongraded. Although some faculty will question the academic legitimacy of Seminar, it can be argued that any course that teaches skills and information, however preparatory, is worthy of credit. Pragmatically, students are not likely to take a course for which there is no external reward.

Although a nongraded course may reduce students' anxieties, holding to the traditional grading system in Seminar forces the class and instructor to deal with issues surrounding grading. If college policy allows students to opt for graded or nongraded approaches in each course, it may be wise for this option to be available in Seminar as well.

Who teaches Seminar depends not only on who is interested and available, but also on decisions about the potential effectiveness of different groups. Faculty members will be most effective if their professional interests are not too far afield from the goals and content of Seminar. Even if a limited number of faculty actually teach Seminar, others will probably be willing and able to participate in the program as guest speakers and resource persons.

Student personnel workers and counselors, whose training is in helping students with academic and personal problems, are the most logical source of Seminar teachers. If they, as a group, are reluctant to take on the task, they are probably making certain assumptions about preconditions for effecting change in clients. When able to view Seminar teaching as preventive outreach and themselves as agents of personal change in that unaccustomed setting, counselors and other student personnel professionals can be highly effective teachers of Seminar.

If upperclassmen teach Seminar, they will need extensive training, close supervision, and the awarding of credit, all of which are costly. Although freshmen may enjoy and find immediately satisfying contact with upperclassmen, sole reliance on upperclassmen teachers of Seminar robs the freshman of a chance to establish relationships with an adult authority figure; interacting with an adult in authority is an important process in Freshman Seminar.

Graduate students in the helping professions are a likely source of Seminar instructors. Freshmen tend to see them as adults, and they themselves will see their role as an integral part of their own professional development. Their only drawback may be their unfamiliarity with the college in which Seminar is offered; additional training sessions for them are therefore indicated.

The planning committee must also decide whether students should be grouped in Seminar sections according to major or career interest. A homogeneous group seems to allow for a more focused curriculum, but a heterogeneous group lends itself to richer and more open discussion of career choice. A mix of homogeneous and heterogeneous sections would make it possible to evaluate the advantages and disadvantages of each type.

3
The Content Areas of Freshman Seminar

In chapter 1, we pointed to three needs experienced by incoming students: the need for information, for competence in the skills of studenthood, and for the attitude of seeing oneself as the active force in one's learning. These three needs can be broadly translated into areas of content—the curricular components, if you will, of Freshman Seminar. This chapter discusses these three content areas. Chapter 4 looks at how the instructor deals methodologically with content. The materials presented in chapter 6 and the classroom narratives in chapter 7 extensively illustrate what actually happens in Seminar classes.

It would be foolhardy to say that either information, skills, or attitude is most important in Seminar. All three are inextricably combined. Skills in studying, say, do not inevitably flow from a sense of self as an active learner, nor does having information in itself lead to competence in skills. Helping students in one of these content areas is likely to yield incremental gains in another area. Successful test-taking behavior, for example, can increase a student's self-confidence in other areas of his life. It may even lead him to seek and to use information more actively.

In Freshman Seminar we do tend to operate behavioristically. That is, we ask students to talk about *what they do* as students, to consider *how* what they do helps or hinders their learning, and to develop alternative ways of *doing*. This emphasis does not preclude discussion of feelings, but it focuses upon actions to which feelings are attached. Insight may or may not occur; changes in ways of *doing things* are what is intended. This is the difference between group therapy, the T-group, the rap session, on the one hand, and Freshman Seminar. It is not a black-and-white distinction, but a difference in emphasis. If students gain insight in Freshman Seminar, it comes from talking and doing things about their own behavior in the college setting.

Information

What information is relevant in Freshman Seminar? There is, first of all, the mass of college policies and procedures; these are, in effect, the laws of the new land that its immigrants—freshmen—must become acquainted with. Unfortunately, ignorance of these laws does not excuse one from following them. The written rules are, with some searching and not a little guidance, easy enough to unearth from college brochures, guidebooks, and catalogs. The unwritten rules, which include ways of safely transgressing the written ones, are learned through personal experience and the shared experience of others. The Seminar can help students gain both kinds of information.

Seminar instructors are often surprised when their students are so receptive to information. But if we put ourselves in the students' place for a moment, it is hardly surprising that in their bewilderment in a new environment, they hunger to reduce their ignorance by knowing something for sure, something written down, about which there seems to be little ambiguity. How they *use* the information to their own advantage will interest them only after they become confident that there *is* order in this new place, that order is often symbolized by the written rules and regulations.

Information seems to be the most immediate, as well as the most easily met, need of students in Seminar. In presenting information, we may want to stress only those facts immediately usable to students. But that is a miscalculation of students' readiness. Students will request information that they will act upon much later in the semester—for example, how to declare a major. We should respond to these requests, for they bespeak the students' overall sense of disorder; students will "use" any information given early in the semester—practically usable or not—at another level to reduce their sense of disorder.

Going Beyond the Information

Rules, alas, are not immutable. People make them and people change them. Moreover, people stretch the rules in enforcing them, and people find ways around them. How do we help students to find out about changes in rules, or to prepare them to do something about changing them? First of all, by letting them know where the rules come from. What person or committee made the deadline for withdrawing from a course without penalty? What was the reasoning behind the creation of this deadline? Whose interests does the rule serve? These are all questions that should be encouraged in Seminar; they go well beyond the simple recounting of information.

Sometimes students' needs for information alone seem bottomless. There is a compulsive, distrusting quality to this need to know every detail (as if all were knowable), and after a few sessions into the semester, it is time-consuming and unprofitable for the instructor to give in to it. At this point, informing students about *sources* of information is useful. For it keeps them from viewing the instructor as the fount of all information and reinforces the notion that information is to be sought out, not merely supplied. "Why didn't they tell me?" students will say when they've run afoul of college rules. "You didn't ask," is the instructor's fair reply. This is the juncture at which informational content and attitudinal content meet.

Besides the instructor, the most immediately available source of information may be right in the classroom—other students:

—*Student:* Do I have to take a foreign language to graduate?
—*Instructor:* Try asking the rest of the class.
—*Student:* Okay. Does anybody know?
—*Student 2:* Yes, if you're in a B.A. program.
—*Student 3:* No, if you've had four years of a foreign language in high school.
—*Student:* Well, I *am* in a B.A. program, and I *did* have four years of Spanish, but not all in high school.
—*Student 2:* Then maybe you don't have to take any more.
—*Student:* How do I find out?

To a point, the students have been helpful here. The student who asked the question, however, is now at an impasse. The instructor can coach him to seek validation of the information he has been given; where did his helpful peers get *their* information? In so doing, the instructor is teaching how to seek information. That process includes checking more than one source of information, validating the sources, and, finally, using the information to meet the particular student's needs.

As a content area of Seminar instruction, information can be a much more enriching focus than it might seem at first. Information is not merely presented; it is discussed, sought out, and yields the kind of action assignment presented in detail on pp. 53-55.

Each college has its own particularly relevant body of information that may be useful to entering freshmen. The listing below is intended to suggest the range of information that might, at one time or another through the semester, be presented in Freshman Seminar:

- Deadline for dropping a course
- Procedure for withdrawing from college
- Policy with regard to cutting classes
- Procedure for appealing a grade
- Deadline for making up an uncompleted course
- Helping services: tutoring, counseling, advising
- Number of academic credits required for graduation
- Number of academic credits for major and minor
- Courses required for liberal arts degree
- Courses required for major/minor
- Governance structure of the college
- Minimum average for Dean's List
- Minimum credit load for financial aid eligibility
- Necessary average for retention and nonprobation

Skills

The successful learner is not necessarily aware that he puts certain skills to work as a learner. The purpose of scholastic skills training in Seminar is, first, to make students aware that there are indeed discrete skills that can be worked on and improved, particularly in the formal educational system of a college. Students are very likely to have developed their skills without having given much thought to them. It is often a revelation, therefore, for students to discover that they "have" something that they didn't know they had!

The beauty of considering skills in Seminar is that it enables students to demystify the learning process, to look upon learning, for the moment, as an assemblage of tasks. Although this may indeed be illusory, it is a helpful illusion, for it makes manageable for the student what might otherwise seem overwhelming. A corresponding drawback in teaching scholastic skills is that the student may tend to regard competency in one skill as an end in itself. He may take magnificent notes but fail his exams; or he may study skillfully but get thrown by multiple choice questions. What the instructor must emphasize is that skills are only tools, that one uses them to achieve certain results. If competency in one skill gives pleasure, so much the better; but if it fails to yield a better grade, say, then the student must look to deficiencies in other skills if he wants to achieve his overall goal.

What skills do we attempt to cover in Freshman Seminar? What do college students do *as students* to learn their course material? Let's start in the classroom. Students *listen to* instructors—not a very observable activity, but an important one nevertheless. They *take notes* on classroom lectures and discussions. They *participate* verbally in class: they ask questions, offer opinions, and respond to questions or comments by other students and the instructor. After classes, students engage in vague activity called *studying,* which supposedly becomes more focused when they are *preparing for examinations.* And the final step occurs when they *take the examinations* that are intended to assess the degree to which particular material has been learned. All of the italicized words and phrases in this paragraph point to separate skills that are appropriate for consideration in Freshman Seminar.

Several other skills are ancillary to, but not included in, the above listing. These are *decision making* and *time management.* They provide the springboard for one's academic activities and should be taught in connection with particular decisions to be made or specific amounts of time to be arranged.

Setting Priorities for Skills Teaching

Depending on how much time is allotted to Seminar, the instructor will set priorities as to which skills and in what depth he wishes to deal with them. One consideration is the extent to which certain skills are taught in places other than Seminar. Speaking in classroom situations, for example, may be taught at a study-skills center. Some consideration can be given, too, to what students say their skill needs are, although given their unfamiliarity with college demands, they may give short shrift to skills that, like class participation, require assertion on their part. They will openly acknowledge a need for task-oriented skills, such as note-taking. The setting of the Seminar agenda, in other words, should be a cooperative venture between students and the instructor.

Textbooks

Textbooks and handbooks on scholastic skills, or what have more recently been called "survival skills," are available in abundance to students and teachers of Seminar. Some, such as Gerow and Lyng's *How to Succeed in College* and Crafts and Hauther's *Surviving the Undergraduate Jungle,* can be used without an accompanying course.[5] Others, such as Weigand and Blake's *College Orientation* are designed either for group instruction or for individual student use.[6] Morgan and Deese's *How to Study* and Millman and Pauk's *How to Take Tests* contain more comprehensive material on particular skills areas.[7] Students should be told that such books exist and can be helpful; but making any text required for Seminar seems valuable only for the dubious reason that students expect a course to have a book. The Seminar instructor can better design his own materials to fit the amount of time available in Seminar and the extent to which he feels it necessary to deal with a particular skill. Unfortunately students and teachers tend to "make the text the authority" when a text is required.

All of the skills-teaching texts we have examined are insensitive to what skills college freshmen may have already developed. Consideration of the here-and-now self seems, unfortunately, limited to those admirable books that deal deal not with scholastic skills, but with values and attitudes, such as Simon's *Values Clarification.*[8] Hence, the instructor must supply this missing element. He must help his Seminar students be aware that after completing twelve years of schooling, they have come to college with some learning strengths and capabilities. Too often freshmen meet instructors and other students who tell them, in effect, "forget everything you've learned, this college business is brand new to you." Indeed it is new, but it is also in part familiar, and it makes psychological sense to help students see college as a *continuation* of their studenthood, albeit in a new and more intellectually demanding environment. In other words, the skills a student has already developed must be acknowledged, be assessed, and then be adapted and expanded to meet the college's more strenuous demands.

A Sequence of Questions for Skills Sessions

When approaching the teaching of a scholastic skill, the instructor will want, first, to find out from students how they *now perform* that skill. What do they do when they take notes? How do they participate in classes? Then, when he finds out what students are now doing, the instructor must ask how well it works. How well has it worked in the past? What can be done to add to or sharpen these skills to make them work better? The answers to this last question will come not only from the instructor but from other students as well.

Students can then practice the new techniques or behaviors, either in class or in a homework assignment. Finally, an assessment can be made of the effectiveness of these new actions. The sequence of questions and procedures outlined here can be applied to the teaching of any skill. The sequence itself should be made explicit. Even if the full sequence is followed with only one skill, students will then have a complete model of skill learning that they can then apply by themselves outside of and after Freshman Seminar.

Fostering Self-Confidence: The Active Learner

In contrast to the informational and skills areas of Seminar content, helping students to see themselves as active learners seems less amenable to directive teaching. The general sense of self-worth is established early in life, engendered by the many ways parents and others have of helping or hindering the child's trust in his own mind and body. According to Erik Erikson and other developmental psychologists, new life experiences tend to arouse earlier doubts about the self. Even Harvard College students, the intellectually privileged, apparently suffer doubts about their competencies when they face the challenges that their previous academic successes have led them to.[9] Thus we can expect that entering college will bring on fresh attacks of self-doubt in many students, even in the scholastically competent.

These doubts are often presented to counselors as feelings of intellectual incapacity. Some students may mask these doubts by making hostile attacks on the college system itself, which they see as the most apparent and immediate cause of self-doubt. Others may respond by withdrawing from the academic pursuit, but without leaving the college; that is, they cut classes, flee from instructors and peers, and fail to complete assignments. Freshmen in a Seminar class are likely to exhibit all of these incipient responses. If we regard these responses as normal for people in a new and unfamiliar setting, then we can set our sights toward helping students over this predictable hurdle of self-doubt. The Seminar offers a haven where students can find out that many other students share their concern, that it is not abnormal, and that focused activity as students will help ease these feelings into the background.

The instructor must be patient with what may seem at times a rampant negativism among his students. Rebuilding the students' sense of themselves as active learners takes time and depends upon their cumulative experience with the new environment. The unknown, for a freshman, can be expected to weigh more heavily than the known. So in Seminar, rather that countering students' self-doubts with injunctions to "think positively," we offer some tools that will—slowly and steadily—yield some success. Finding out information about the college and practicing the skills necessary for academic work are two major activities that can shore up students' sense of self-worth. For a very vulnerable student, particularly one who indeed lacks scholastic skills, this can be a delicate process. One failure can send him into a spiral of self-doubt that will lead to other failures. But, on the other hand, a single success—if acknowledged, shared with others, and praised—may provide the self-esteem upon which other successes can be built.

Everything a Seminar instructor does is directed toward the goal of students seeing themselves as active learners who are not simply at the mercy of the institution. The instructor provides support by being a faithful proponent of their success: he makes student expressions of self-doubt allowable, he helps students to listen to one another, to take one another seriously, he applauds their accomplishments and he acknowledges their failures. He helps students understand that they already have skills and strengths. He must own up to their skills and strengths and guide them to use the skills they *do* have adaptively at the college.

The harsh reality upon which personal value is conferred in college is quite narrowly conditional, and students know this. They are judged academically by their own products: their papers, lab reports, examinations. No one in authority gives them a good grade for being pleasant or even for their academic effort. This is naturally frightening to a student who has previously been valued for these other, non-academic reasons. And though a Seminar instructor can be sympathetic to a student whose niceness has paid off in the past, he must make it clear that the old rules do not apply, all the while providing concrete support for the student to work productively under the new rules of academic competence.

Summary

The three curricular components of Freshman Seminar are information, skills, and attitude toward studenthood. For the instructor's convenience, these three components can be considered separately, though in practice they are inextricably connected during class sessions.

The Seminar approach tends to be behavioristic. All three curricular components are dealt with in the context of what students *do:* how they *seek* and *use* information; how they *perform* the scholastic skills; and what they *do* in response to their attitudes. This emphasis differentiates Freshman Seminar from insight-oriented groups such as T-groups and from unstructured groups such as rap groups.

Information

The Seminar provides information on the written policies and procedures of the college as well as on the unwritten rules that are learned from one's peers. Freshmen are likely to be eager consumers of information, particularly early in their first semester; instructors should understand that the students' "information hunger" is a way of reducing their sense of disorder.

Seminar sessions do much more than give information. Students must investigate the source of information, the rationale for policies and procedures, ways of changing them, and ways of using the information. It is the instructor's job to wean students from viewing him as *the* source of college information; he does this by sending them to other sources and by using the members of the Seminar as an abundant source of information.

Skills

Skills-teaching attempts to make the student's work more manageable by focusing on specific areas of behavior. Separate Seminar sessions can be offered in listening, class participation, note-taking, studying, preparing for exams, taking exams, making decisions, and managing time. The selection of skills topics should take account of what other courses or out-of-class offerings are already available at the college. While Seminar students should have some chance to choose the skills they wish to cover in the Seminar, the instructor must also add skills areas that students may not be aware they will need.

Textbooks on study skills and student guides for college survival can provide useful material in Seminar. If a text is required, however, both students and the instructor may become dependent on the book, and the instructor will be less likely to develop materials directly relevant to the particular institution. Moreover, most texts fail to help students see that their college experience is a *continuation* of their previous schooling.

In teaching scholastic skills, an instructor should offer students a training process that can be used beyond the Seminar. This process begins with eliciting from students how they now perform a particular skill, moves to their consideration of how well their skills are working, and leads to suggestions for changing skills behaviors. Students are then asked to practice the new behaviors in Seminar simulations as well as in assignments in other classes.

Fostering Attitudes toward Active Learning

When they enter college, many students begin to doubt their intellectual competence. Students may respond to these doubts by withdrawing from full participation in academic life or by attacking the system, which they hold responsible for their discomfort. Seminar instructors can help allay these doubts by encouraging their expression in class and by working on concrete areas (e.g., skills training, seeking and giving information) that will yield greater competence, thus pushing the self-doubts into the background. Since it takes time to change attitudes, the instructor cannot expect his efforts in this direction to be apparent, even within the period of a semester.

If the Seminar allows students to express self-doubt yet works towards competence in skills and in the gaining of information, students will begin to view themselves as active learners. The instructor must make clear, however, that in the academic setting one is judged not by one's efforts, but by one's intellectual competence. This may be a harsh reality for those whose hard work and pleasant demeanor have been rewarded.

4

Methods in Teaching Freshman Seminar

The very word "seminar" tells us something about the format of a continuing orientation course. According to *The American College Dictionary,* a seminar is "a group of advanced students studying under a professor with each doing original research and all exchanging results through reports and discussion."[10] At first blush, it may seem inappropriate for freshmen to be undertaking a course "for advanced students." But as we noted in chapter 3, freshmen, as students, are *advanced,* twelve years advanced into studenthood, and are now at the third level of formal learning, the level we call "higher education." In this sense, then, students who come to Freshman Seminar are advanced. And they should be approached with full acknowledgment that, no matter how deficient they may regard themselves, they have indeed learned much about being students through long experience of schooling.

Do students in Freshman Seminar do "original research?" Yes, in several ways. They research themselves, their behavior as students, their responses to the college setting, and, using the college as an arena for observation, they research the written and unwritten rules of the college. In this sense then, self-observation and self-reporting can be regarded as original: the self is the primary source, and no one else can make that study in the same way. So, indeed, Seminar students *are* researchers, and original ones at that.

Another part of our dictionary definition fits more snugly: "a group . . . exchanging results through reports and discussions." In a seminar all members of the group learn from *sharing* information and ideas. Every member teaches and learns. The instructor—the traditional authority in the classroom—therefore has to change his role. His function is to help the sharing process along, to open up communications among members of the group. Thus, he must play down the authority role in which students will cast him.

There is a very real difficulty in running Freshman Seminar truly as a seminar. For the instructor does have immense authority; not only does he give grades, but he also has information about and experience with the college that his students cannot have. How then is he to convincingly back away from the authority role? The answer is that he doesn't always back away, nor does he consistently act the authority. Authority is passed back and forth between and among the students and instructor, depending upon the subject matter. A student is always an authority about his own feelings and opinions; he alone has them, authors them, as it were, and can express them. He alone is the authority.

When it comes to information about college governance and the like, however, the instructor is the clear authority.

Passing authority around the group is important because it helps to lead students away from the notion that their new environment contains two classes of people: those who know and those who don't. Some know some things, others know other things. The practice of sharing authority can also break another commonly held notion—that those who know keep their knowledge and that those who don't know keep their ignorance. In Seminar, students are encouraged to express their thoughts, whether they perceive themselves as "knowing" or not. Moreover, they are asked to seek out what others know: information, ideas, opinions. That is how a Freshman Seminar group at its best can be a community of learners in which authority is truly shared among members of the group.

An instructor can model the sharing of authority in the way he responds to students' questions. To a question that implies that *he* has the answer, he can reply, "I don't have *the* answer, but I have an opinion, if you'd like to hear it." Or, to a factual question to which there is a factual answer, he can reply, "I do have that information; it's from the introductory chapter of the catalog." Here the instructor is refusing to take credit for having information; he is letting the students know that he, too, has to *get* information, that he, too, hasn't the answers to all questions.

The Sequence of Session Topics: Readiness

In what sequence Seminar topics should be discussed is not a trivial question. Students to some extent face similar problems at given times during the semester. How ready they are to be engaged in a particular topic depends on how much commonality and immediacy that specific topic arouses.

The group's readiness is by no means easy to assess. But the instructor, even at the outset of the semester, can elicit and evaluate some sense of the group's interest in a particular topic.[11] Thus, he must know what events might be pressing upon his students, e.g., exams, fraternity rushing, deadlines. The trick is to select topics that will be valuable in the next few weeks, yet that are already felt by students to be looming up. By the seventh week of the semester, for example, midterm examinations will be impending. The instructor will have to raise anticipatory anxieties by polling the class: "How many have midterms next week? How many the week after next? Maybe next session would be a good time to deal with exam-taking skills." The instructor is likely to get general assent. If he waits until exams are already under way, the students might be too anxious for calm discussion. If he waits until exams are over, whatever help the discussion might have provided will have been lost. The instructor must therefore not only be aware of what events are coming up; he sometimes must also make suggestions for scheduling topics when the Seminar group fails to do so.

Group-Utilizing Techniques

Teaching strategies for group interaction are outlined in James R. Davis's *Teaching Strategies for the College Classroom.*[12] A rich collection of exercises for groups learning group problem-solving techniques has been gathered by Pfeiffer and Jones in their two volumes, *Handbook of Structured Experiences for Human Relations Training.*[13] Although these exercises are not directly relevant to the academic focus of Freshman Seminar, they can be readily adapted to the topics covered in Seminar. The classroom lesson plans presented in chapter 6 of this book lean heavily on techniques suggested by the Pfeiffer and Jones exercises.

Seating Arrangements in Seminar

Where and how group members sit can do much to foster or hinder group interaction. The traditional classroom is arranged for traditional leader/follower interaction: students sit in parallel rows facing the separate and sometimes raised seat of the instructor. Students are expected to sit in their assigned places, the instructor in his. In a conference room, the seating arrangement is different: members of the group sit around a table so that they can hear and see one another directly. Every member has easy access to every other member, although all are expected to gather around the conference table.

In Freshman Seminar, face-to-face arrangements are necessary, together with the flexibility in subdividing the group that only a room with *movable* chairs can provide. A conference room is not desirable; the long table prevents paired interaction and is usually too heavy to move out of the way.

If all members of a Seminar group sit in a circle, they can see and hear one another. Since college classrooms cannot usually be reserved for exclusive Seminar use, students will probably have to rearrange the chairs into a circle each time the class meets. This in itself is a group-fostering circumstance, for it forces students actively to remake their group setting at each class. For the first three or four class sessions, the instructor may have to remind students about the circle. We tend to "take things as we find them," to leave the chairs in the traditional leader/follower pattern. But when students take the lead in moving chairs, it is a good indication that the group-centered norm for Seminar has taken hold. Surely, some students, particularly those who get to class late, will want to sit behind the circle. For their convenience, and to enforce the single-chair arrangement, it is wise to put enough chairs in the circle to seat the entire class, even though some members may be absent. That way a latecomer will not be able to take, literally, a back seat, but must join his peers in the circle.

Even in the circular setting, students have ways of maintaining their accustomed distance from the instructor. If the instructor is seated when students arrive for class, they may well leave one or even two empty seats on either side of him. This strategy can be foiled; the instructor simply waits to take his seat until the students are seated. Or he can simply ask students to take seats on either side of him, saying, "Hey, I need company over here!"

Students do tend to take the same seats class after class, next to peers they feel most comfortable with. The instructor can occasionally jumble this arrangement so that students will gain an overall comfort in the group. A new seat, trivial as it may seem, changes the fixed positions that students seek and tend to settle into.

Pairing

One-to-one interactions are usually less threatening than a student's participation in the larger group. In a larger group, moreover, an individual member has greater opportunity to remain passive; in a twosome at least some response from the less active member is required. Pairing students up in Seminar can be useful as a foundation for larger group interaction. In pairs, students are likely to share ideas and opinions that they are not yet ready to express in the full group.

Pairing students is meant to foster communication. But instructions about the content of their interaction must be explicit; otherwise, you will have pairs sitting silently together, looking like couples on a mismatched blind date. It helps, too, to put on the board the intended subject of their discussion; the pairs can then refer to the board without bringing the instructor into their twosome.

Pairing is also one of several methods by which data can be gathered *for* the entire group, *from* each member of the group. After spending some time in pairs, therefore, the total class group must meet to "report out" the data the pairs have collected. Making the transition from the pairs to the total group can be bridged by having each member of a twosome report his partner's contribution. This tends to help students listen to their partners; it is also generally more comfortable than reporting out one's *own* points.

Lest this whole procedure of pairing sound overprotective, it should be said that these methods are used when the instructor senses that the students are reluctant to open up in the large group. This is likely to occur early in the semester, but not exclusively then, for there are issues raised throughout the semester that may nearly silence an otherwise active class. In a discussion of study behavior, for example, students may be quite ready to share quantitative information such as how many hours a week they study; questions about where they study can raise uneasiness, which may call for a shift from the total group to the pairs.

Individual Data Collection for Group Sharing

Another method for collecting data from each student is the "unfinished statement." The instructor simply asks each student to complete a statement put on the board. "What can make me uneasy in class is ________," or, "I like (or don't like) the kind of teacher who ________." Students can also be asked to collect information outside of class, again using a written device, one example of which would be the week-long time sheet for recording one's hourly use of time.

Like pairing, the strategies that ask students to *write down* their contributions are intended to make it easier for them to participate. Most students find it initially easier to read what they have written rather than to "speak off the top of their heads." Furthermore, the request to write something down somehow seems to be taken more seriously than a request for an oral contribution. If the instructor then transcribes on the board what students have written and shared orally, this too seems to amplify the seriousness of what they have produced. Their thoughts do not just disappear in the air; they are on the blackboard for all to see and read.

Role Playing

When students report problems involving other people, role playing can help them to see and work on their own behavior. Role playing seems appropriate when other, more traditional ways of understanding a problem lead to a stalemate. In other words, it is wise to wait until the nondramatized question-and-answer method gets you nowhere before you launch into role playing. Here is an example:

—*Student:* This teacher just doesn't like me.

—*Instructor:* What does he do that makes you think that?
—*Student:* No matter what I write for him, it's not good enough. He just criticizes.
—*Student 2:* Have you had a conference with him?
—*Student:* Yes, and he doesn't let me get a word in edgewise.
—*Student 2:* Can't you tell him what *you* think about your own work?
—*Student:* Yes, I've tried, but he doesn't want to hear it. That's why I think he just doesn't like me.

There is a standoff here. The student is nowhere near taking any advice from his fellow student, who may indeed not be asking the right questions. We need to know more about what goes on between the student and the instructor he feels dislikes him. Role playing may help.

—*Instructor:* Okay, Jerry, we now know something about how you see this teacher. Don, you be the teacher, as Jerry has described him, in a conference with Jerry. You've just let him have it about his paper. Jerry, you're Jerry. Let's see what happens.
—*Don:* Jerry, this is a miserable paper. The ideas are disorganized, the grammar is atrocious, and . . .
—*Jerry:* But can't you . . .
—*Don:* And I don't understand your . . .
—*Jerry:* (louder) But what is . . . what is disorganized about my first paragraph?
—*Don:* (pauses to read it over) Well . . . the first sentence I'll grant you is clear enough though not very exciting. You could have used a better word for "awesome" and . . .
—*Jerry:* Okay, but the paragraph isn't disorganized, right, whatever else may be wrong with it.
—*Don:* No, it's not disorganized, I'll say that, but you've got many other errors here which . . .
—*Instructor:* Okay, cut. Now Jerry, you *did* get a word in edgewise. How'd you manage that?
—*Jerry:* Don was different from that teacher.
—*Don:* I was being as belligerent as I could, Jerry; you were just persistent, that's all.
—*Instructor:* What did the rest of the class notice about how Jerry acted in this situation?

Role playing is here extended just long enough to elicit dramatic behavior that students can discuss. Jerry got some practice in being more direct and insistent than he had been in his actual conferences with his teacher. The role-playing Don nicely rewarded Jerry for his persistence. Whether Jerry's assertiveness in this simulation can be transferred to the real situation is an open question; role playing assumes that rehearsing desired behavior can help in this respect. At least Jerry knows he can interrupt an authority when he feels it is necessary.

Many interpersonal situations relevant to the college setting can be productively and enjoyably role-played in Seminar. Here is a very abbreviated list of such situations that might come up:

- getting an appointment with a teacher/department advisor/dean; student/secretary role play
- clarifying an assignment; student/instructor
- responding to a request to lend a notebook/paper to someone; student/student
- requesting quiet for studying; student/parent, student/sibling, student/student
- asking for reconsideration of a grade; student/instructor
- responding to a request to take off for a weekend; student/nonstudent peer, student/parent
- responding to a request to join a club, college committee, etc.; student/student, student/faculty member
- getting acquainted with others socially; student/student

Most of these situations call for the role-playing principles to face the perceived authority of an adult or a peer. Since, as we have noted in chapter 3, this seems to be a major difficulty for entering students, role playing is highly appropriate for helping them find their own resources in dealing with authority. When students simply lack information, role playing is not called for. But when students need some dramatic way of viewing their own behavior and can allow others to see it in classroom simulation, role playing is useful.

What does the rest of the class do during a role-playing session? They must be told that they, too, have a part in this process—as careful observers and, later, as commentators on the main action. Role playing situations, if chosen to tap the potential feelings of a majority of the class members, will engage the observers without much direction from the instructor. A student's response to a death in his family, for example, is probably too heavy and too remote from the experience of others in the class to be appropriate for role playing.

Individual Problem Solving in Seminar

It does not take long for Seminar students to view the class as a place where they can air their problems as college students. These problems have a personal, individual tone; but rarely are they so idiosyncratic that they cannot be related to and helpful for many others in the Seminar. An instructor must make a quick judgment as to whether the student's problem is appropriate for class discussion; it can be aired then and there, deferred to a later class session, or reserved for a private discussion between student and instructor. Generally, we can assume that a student who presents a problem situation during Seminar is looking for help from other Seminar members as well as from the instructor. We should not assume, however, that the class is ready or willing to deal with that particular problem or that the instructor is. A convenient rule of thumb is: how comfortable do most of the class and the instructor seem to feel about discussing a particular student's problem? If a distressed student announces to the class that she is pregnant—even though this may be a problem many students have thought about and might be comfortable about discussing in other settings—a discussion of it in Seminar would probably cause confusion about the nature of Seminar. The instructor cannot, of course, ignore the student who drops this bombshell. He can, however, welcome her to a private discussion of the matter, and other students who want to help may approach her outside of class.

But what about individual problems that *are* amenable to Seminar discussion? Dealing with them at some length will admittedly throw the Seminar syllabus off schedule, which is good reason for leaving some sessions open in the syllabus, or designated for follow-up. The instructor has to judge whether a discussion of a particular student's problem will be of value to the class as a whole. Is it a problem that others are encountering or might encounter? True, the problem may not be immediately relevant to the entire group, but the process of resolving the problem may indeed be valuable to many more students than the one who presents it. In addition, a discussion of an individual problem may raise side issues that can be interesting and useful for the group as a whole.

For example, Gina comes into a Seminar class saying something is "not fair." She works afternoons, needs special permission to register for an all-morning class schedule, but will be limited to twelve credits unless she has a B average or better. Since she's a first-semester freshman, she doesn't yet *have* an average, though she reports doing better than B work in all her courses. How, she asks, can she get her needed schedule and still take the sixteen credits she wants?

—*Gina:* It isn't fair to the freshman, this rule. Why'd they make it anyhow? Aren't we grown up enough to decide how many credits we can manage?
—*Instructor:* Maybe it would help to find out from the people who made the rule.
—*Gina:* Fine, I'd like to see it changed, or find out how I can get around it. There must be some way!
—*Jerry:* (to instructor) Who *does* make this rule?
—*Instructor:* This one is made by a Senate committee on Undergraduate Regulations. See the chairman, Professor Engles,

Gina, to find out more about it.
—*Larry:* Gina, if there's a rule like this, there's bound to be a good reason for it.
—*Jerry:* You mean she shouldn't try to fight it? No rule is without exceptions or ways around it. I'm all for Gina seeing the chairman.
—*Larry:* But why hassle it? You won't get anywhere. You'll just get more frustrated.
—*Instructor:* Has anyone here ever challenged a rule that didn't seem fair to your own situation?
—*Laura:* Yeah, in high school, they wouldn't let me go home for lunch period. I knew a door I could escape through without anybody knowing, so I just did it.
—*Jimmy:* But that's not challenging a rule. It's just finding your own way around it.
—*Instructor:* Okay. We've said there are at least two ways of getting your way in the face of a rule you think unfair. One is by seeing the people who make the rules. Another is by quietly disobeying them.
—*Gina:* Well, I'd like to know how I can get around this one.
—*Larry:* If you just registered for twelve credits now and added another course later, would anyone find out?
—*Gina:* I wonder. (to instructor) Would they?
—*Instructor:* You'd be taking a risk. What do you think would be the consequences if someone found out?
—*Gina:* They'd just not let me take those extra four credits, I suppose. So I'd be back where I started from.
—*Laura:* But it's not like plagiarizing, not something serious like that!
—*Instructor:* What we are doing is anticipating the consequences of an action. When you consider alternative actions, it makes sense to consider the alternative consequences.
—*Gina:* What might happen, then, if I went to see Professor Engles?
—*Laura:* He could say, "Sorry, that's the rule, no exceptions."
—*Larry:* Or if you showed him you've got a B average so far, maybe he'd let you take more than twelve credits.
—*Gina:* But I don't have any final grades yet.
—*Larry:* Don't you have your mid-term exams and papers? Couldn't you bring him those?
—*Gina:* Sounds like a good idea. Or I could get notes from my teachers saying I'm running B's and A's.
—*Instructor:* Okay, why don't you try that and report back to us what happens.

The issues this particular problem raises engage the entire group in problem solving and yield a number of broadly relevant questions for all students. How do we view rules? How does one go about testing their applicability to oneself? What are the advantages of simply disobeying a rule as against appealing it at its source? Surely the class does not take any of these issues to any great depths. But they have been touched upon, can be returned to in later classes, and, in the process, a student is being helped to find a procedure for resolving her special problem.

The Action Assignment

The classroom method for handling an individual problem has been suggested in the above illustration. Gina will report her visit to Professor Engles back to the Seminar group the following week. The instructor may ask her to write a narrative of her encounter with the professor. In this way, she will have to do some thinking about the problem she presented to the class. The written assignment brings some closure to the event and, we hope, will help Gina to see it not only as a problem to be resolved, but also as part of her own continuing interaction with the people and policies that make up the college environment.

This is one example of the action assignment, one that grows quite spontaneously out of discussion in the Seminar classroom. The action assignment calls for students, individually or in groups, to take some action in the college world outside of the Seminar. Action assignments can be given to one student, as with Gina, or, on the heels of a full class session on a given topic, to every class member. A session on participating in class, for example, can end with the assignment that every student speak up in a class he hasn't spoken in. Further examples of action assignments and how they grow out of the discussion in Seminar can be found in the classroom dialogues in chapter 8.

The action assignment forges links between what happens within the Seminar class and what happens in the college world outside. It is a necessary counterforce to the protected and non-threatening atmosphere that is often engendered in a Seminar group. Some continuing orientation programs like Freshman Seminar make action assignments a focal point of the program. At Kent State University, continuing orientation students are required to interview one college official, visit one college office or department, and attend one extracurricular activity. They then write reports of these experiences on prepared sheets provided by the instructors. They must complete these action assignments in order to pass the Kent State course.

Action assignments should not be made casually or vaguely. For Gina's assignment, we did not just suggest that she "see Professor Engles." Nor did the other students give Gina a tight sequence of questions to ask, though this might have been formulated through a role-play simulation of her intended visit to the professor. But Gina will see Professor Engles with a strategy suggested by her peers; she will go armed with papers and exams from her classes or with notes from her teachers. In other words, she isn't going empty-handed or empty-headed. Similarly, Seminar students can come up with questions and strategies that they anticipate would be helpful in an action assignment. Some of this preliminary planning may be of little use once the student is out "in the field." But that is not to say the planning is worthless, for students who *do* have a plan are less likely to feel at the mercy of the field situation, even if that plan has to be changed on the spot. Here is one example:

A Seminar student assigned to interview the dean of students had prepared herself by writing pages of questions, with plenty of empty lines in between for the expected answers. Having not the slightest idea what a dean of students did or was, she assumed the dean was a student, a kind of student leader. When she arrived at the carpeted office for her interview, she was surprised to find that the dean was a woman of middle age. But that didn't stop the student from asking her first prepared question: "What year of college are you in?" When the dean told her she hadn't been a student in years, the student said, "I didn't think a student would get an office like this!" and flipped through her notebook for more appropriate questions. All of this she reported in her narrative of the interview; her embarrassment was momentary, and she was glad to have a written plan to refer to.

Other Devices

Some structural aids help students to be more generally aware of the continuity of their academic lives. For example a calendar for the entire semester can be provided, a calendar in which students have to put due dates for papers and exams, college deadlines, and holidays. Or a weekly journal, unstructured but focused on school-related matters, can be assigned. This latter structural device naturally promotes more personalized discussion in class (a calendar's yield tends to be much tamer). Whatever the choice of device, some assigned, overall organizer can be a great help to entering students. It reinforces the notion that being a student is a complex business, full of scheduled events and responsibilities that should not be left to chance remembering. The executive has a secretary; the student has to be his own secretary. Keeping track of his life and the necessary interactions with his environment can help him become his own secretary during his first semester at college.

Summary

The term "seminar" holds the key to the overall teaching method in Freshman Seminar. The instructor facilitates the students' own research into their lives as students and helps open up communication so that students can express themselves and understand the others.

The Seminar format implies that group members and the instructor share authority. This method can help students to alter their notions about authority, notions to the effect that some have authority and some do not and that authority cannot be passed around. An instructor can model the sharing of authority by explicitly differentiating his opinions from facts, and by making clear his dependence upon sources for information.

Instructors may find many techniques useful for fostering interaction in the Seminar class. A *circular seating arrangement* that allows for flexibility and face-to-face accessibility is desirable. *Pairing* students for one-to-one dialogues can often help students to generate material for sharing later with the total class group. Asking students to *complete unfinished statements* is another way of collecting data quickly, with the advantage that students may find it easier to write down opinions first than to talk glibly. *Role playing* can be useful when a student's problems in interpersonal situations require dramatization in order for him to see his own behavior. In most such role-plays, the student faces the authority of a peer or an adult; rehearsing these situations can help students find their own resources in dealing with authority.

Seminar students naturally bring individual problems for consideration by the Seminar group. The instructor must judge how appropriately the group can deal with an individual problem; that is, he can assess how comfortable the class will be in discussing it and the extent to which the rest of the class shares the same problem. A quite specific problem may, however, be a springboard for discussion of issues of importance to the whole class.

Action assignments call for students to do something outside the classroom to practice what they have learned in Seminar. These assignments arise out of class discussion; they can be made individually or to all members of the Seminar.

Students can be helped to view their academic lives more coherently when the Seminar uses organizing devices, e.g., a weekly journal and a semester's calendar. These devices reinforce the seriousness and purposiveness that successful studenthood requires.

5
Staff Development

The previous chapters have included much in the way of direct guidance to the Seminar instructor. This chapter is addressed to the coordinator or director of a Freshman Seminar program. We assume that instructors will need and want opportunities to discuss with colleagues their approaches and experiences with their groups. What generally these needs are and how the coordinator can meet them is the subject of this chapter.

Limitations of Previous Training Backgrounds

The Freshman Seminar instructor does both teaching and counseling. This is a difficult task for one trained in either discipline. Teachers tend to use direct methods, are accustomed to presenting information, and are not generally adept at fading into the background during class discussion. Counselors, on the other hand, particularly those trained in nondirective methods, tend to allow a wider range of expression from students and, if untrained in group processes, to focus more on the individual student than on the group or on what group members have in common.

Though these differences may be overstated, the point is that a Seminar staff made up of both teachers and counselors will probably have people from both ends of the continuum. If the staff is faculty only, the training will probably focus on loosening up the teacher to deal with students as individuals to allow for greater class participation, and on helping him take an occasional backseat in class discussion. If the staff is all counselors, training will probably call for a tightening up of instructional methods and for helping counselors to close discussions and to feel more comfortable about making clear demands on their students.

But with either counselors or teachers, combining expertise from each background means shuttling back and forth between teaching and counseling methods. In dealing, for example, with grades and grading systems, the instructor must first make a clear factual presentation and follow it with some assessment of how well this is understood. The instructor trained as a teacher is prepared for such tasks. But a follow-up discussion that elicits students' feelings about grades requires some skills that are learned in counseling training: communicating empathy, trust, and genuineness. A teacher-trained Seminar instructor may have some difficulty in this area.

The class formats we present in chapter 6 were designed for a Seminar staff composed almost entirely of trained counselors. The emphasis, therefore, may seem somewhat heavier on the formal and structured aspect of Seminar method, for it was in this area that these instructors needed help. They were already trained to be "good listeners," but they lacked guidance in the partial structuring of Seminar sessions so that they could cover many topic areas within the realities of a one-day-a-week, semester-long course. In mounting a training program, it is essential to know the backgrounds of your staff. They will most naturally rely upon the skills they already have, sometimes to the neglect of the alternative skills and methods that Seminar teaching requires.

Counselors' Weak Spots

Instructors trained as counselors may especially resist testing and grading Seminar students. They may plead recurrently that this burden be lifted from them, claiming that it is not appropriate to judge students on the topics we are dealing with. This is nonsense. Students can be tested on the information they learn in Seminar, and by presenting them with hypothetical situations, the instructor can assess how they would *use* that information in making a decision about some area of academic life. They can also be tested and judged in the skills of information gathering. What does make sense in the counselor's plea for eliminating grading in Seminar is that the counselor is trained *not* to test, or at least not to judge, and therefore feels uncomfortable in that role. Staff training must meet this issue head on. One approach that Hunter counselors have found helpful is working out the explicit criteria by which Seminar students are to be judged. Sharing these criteria among staff early in the semester can help to lessen, if not alleviate, the counselor-trained instructor's discomfort about grading.

Generalists vs. Specialists

The broad range of topics included in Freshman Seminar may leave the instructor feeling that he is expected, unfairly, to become an expert in areas well outside his expertise or interest. Surely the Seminar content is not in the traditional range of any one discipline's subject matter. A sociology instructor recruited to teach Seminar will not always relish doing a session on note-taking, though he may bring special skill and interest to a session on speaking up in class. But the Seminar instructor must, at least for the purpose of teaching Seminar, consider himself a generalist in the "general" area of college education. He can call on the special resources of other Seminar instructors to teach his class in areas of their expertise or call on them to teach him how to deal with those areas. But by and large, he is running his own show on the basis of his genuine interest in helping freshmen learn the ropes.

In this age of specialization, it is not always easy to find those willing to take on the generalist role, if even for a few class hours a week. In every nook and cranny of the college, including the counseling center, there are those who have carved out a specialist role for themselves and those whose livelihoods depend on their keeping such specialties to themselves. Although the seminar program may lose if instructors do not consider the teaching of Seminar a key function, it stands to gain by this very state of affairs. Teaching Freshman Seminar is not an activity by which instructors are judged professionally; it therefore can offer some focused diversion from their "regular" work.

Individual Staff Contributions to Seminar Curriculum

Each instructor of course brings his or her own individual style and particular interests into the Seminar. A social scientist may want to differentiate the various social science disciplines; this is particularly appropriate in the pre-planning sessions, where students choose their courses for the following semester. A counselor interested in family therapy may want to run a session on students' changing relations with their parents—an area that may come into play during the sessions on time management or study skills. During the first few semesters of the Seminar's existence, these topics invariably get tried out and may eventually become an accepted part of the Seminar. But this can happen only if, in staff sharing and training sessions, the instructors are encouraged to report on their sessions. A free flow of information is essential. Otherwise, valuable teaching contributions remain the sole possession of a single instructor.

In addition to encouraging the sharing of experience in staff sessions, the coordinator can make written materials available in an easily accessible materials center. A file cabinet will do, clearly marked and with the materials well organized inside. The materials center is not, however, meant to be an alternative to the sharing of materials at the staff meetings. After an instructor describes an innovative session in staff meeting, he is usually encouraged to "write it up," and copies of the report are filed in the materials center file. Even then, instructors have to be reminded about the materials center. When an instructor complains that he "doesn't know what to do with test-taking,"—the coordinator tells him to take a look at the materials center—it often seems to come as a surprise. As an antidote to this, it may make sense to have a Seminar staff bulletin board near the coordinator's office, on which are put up sample copies of all new material coming in, with the notation "more copies in the material center file."

Each instructor himself decides how far afield to go in creating Seminar topics. By "far afield" is meant how peripheral from academically centered concerns. Sexual values and behaviors, for example, may indeed be relevant to many college students; they may be greatly distracting from academic concerns. But it is perhaps an indulgence in the relevant for Seminar to include a session on sexual values. After all, many colleges offer courses on this topic. Dealing with an explosive topic in a classroom is a difficult matter—the more so since Seminar is not a traditional lecture class, but a class that encourages free expression. Peer-group response may not be appropriate in some situations. The seminar, unlike a "rap session" or group therapy, must allow for a modicum of free expression but stick close to the subject of "being a student in this college," a subject that is not generally dealt with in an organized way anywhere *but* in the Seminar.

The Instructor's Involvement with Students' Personal Problems

Because Seminar deals with personal issues and instructors encourage expression of individual problems related to academic life, the student rightly expects the instructor to take some continuing interest in him as a person. One cannot help someone to open up one minute and turn away from him the next. Like any faculty member, therefore, the Seminar instructor must be available to see students outside of class, but with the difference that the student may be coming on a much more personal basis. For instructors trained as counselors this presents no problem; individual consultation is their stock-in-trade. For faculty instructors, we can surmise that they would not take on Seminar work unless they expected this kind of interaction with students. Yet, untrained in personal counseling, faculty instructors may begin to feel the burden of helping students with problems they are not equipped to handle. This is good reason to give faculty instructors a substantial orientation to the college's counseling services before they begin teaching Seminar. If possible, they should be introduced to a few counselors to whom they can make direct referrals if necessary.

The Instructor's Attitude toward the Institution

Seminar instructors, involved as they are in teaching about college student survival, necessarily find themselves teaching about the specific demands of their own institution. They need not and will not necessarily be sympathetic to each and every college policy, nor should they pretend to be. But if an individual instructor disagrees with, say, the foreign language requirement, he ought not to neglect the topic in Seminar, and he might neglect it without being fully aware of it. Staff sessions must therefore include discussion of college policies and regulations that Seminar instructors oppose. It should be emphasized in staff meetings that instructors' opinions presented in Seminar are valuable to students if they lead students to offer their *own* opinions. But if the facts of college policies are not presented, the Seminar student cannot make informed decisions about his life as a college student. In staff sessions, the instructor can play the role of presenting the college policies he disagrees with and can thus take the edge off his discomfort with a particular policy.

If the Seminar instructor presents himself as an overall advocate or as an adversary of the college, he is likely to reinforce whatever preconceptions his students have of him and the college. An angry student may decry a regulation he regards as unfair and expect to enlist the full sympathy of an instructor. What is helpful to the student in this situation is, first, a validation of his own feelings of injustice, and then, an honest search for what the student, not the instructor, can do about the situation. Do others in the class feel the same way about it? What have they done about it? If the college bureaucracy works so slowly that a policy will not be changed until long after it affects the students in the class, how can they face up to it in a way that will cause them a minimum of anguish? An instructor overwhelmed by his own feelings on an issue may not be able to lead a rational, productive discussion on it. In staff training sessions, therefore, one must find out which college policies and regulations instructors oppose, so that their feelings in these areas can be aired outside of the Seminar sessions.

Information for Staff

A staff composed of "old hands" at the college will not require much information about college rules and resources. Periodic reminders and memos from the coordinator will suffice. But Seminar instructors who are new at the college need an intensive staff session to familiarize them with the facts. Unfortunately, there is often so much information that it is not absorbed in this manner. Rather than merely rehearse the facts, a presentation of the *sources* of this information is more helpful: the catalog, the course guide, brochures from various departments and programs. Moreover, directors and deans from the helping services and academic divisions can be brought into staff meetings to present information and answer questions. If hundreds of new students enroll in Freshman Seminar, the heads of programs and services will find it very worthwhile to attend a Seminar staff meeting.

Seminar as Catchall Forum

If the Seminar is run as a catchall forum, a problem arises that is perhaps inherent to any program that succeeds in reaching a large number of students. The coordinator, within a few semesters of the inception of Seminar, may find himself deluged by offers from academic departments, services, library, etc., to send people to speak to the Seminar classes. At first, such requests are flattering; they do indeed mean that the Seminar is known throughout the college. But the coordinator must be highly selective in allowing guest visits to Seminar classes. At the worst, a Seminar can degenerate into a series of guest lecturers; it is not then a Seminar, but a kind of orientation to college, a format that students long ago were forced to endure in compulsory assemblies and chapels. Furthermore, an abundance of visiting lecturers keeps the two main kinds of relationships from building: the relationship between the student and the Seminar instructor, and the sharing relationship among Seminar students. Obviously, outside speakers should not be barred from Seminar. An occasional new face is stimulating to classes, and particular expertise—in career choice, for example—often warrants a presentation by an outsider. But such visitations should be carefully chosen and well spaced.

Most important, they should offer what the instructor himself cannot offer, either for lack of expertise or for lack of inclination.

Planning Together

All tasks undertaken over a set period of time have their ups and downs for those who do them, and teaching Seminar is no exception. The energies of college instructors, like those of the students they teach, seem most taxed during the final weeks of a semester. This may be because the most time-consuming assignments, and the grading of them, are left to the end of the semester. There is no inherent reason why this has to happen in Freshman Seminar. Indeed, instructors can make it easier for themselves and for their students by leveling out the work throughout the semester, by setting deadlines for work every few weeks, and by not overweighing the grade importance of a final exam. Granted, students and Seminar instructors will have other end-of-semester deadlines that cannot be spread out over the semester. In the Seminar, however, this can be avoided through careful group planning from the outset of the term.

Instructors' Own Needs and Expectations

What can instructors expect to get out of teaching Freshman Seminar? It is a novel and peculiar sort of teaching for the teacher, and a novel and peculiar sort of counseling for the counselor. Instructors come from all areas and have somewhat different needs. The faculty member may want contact with students at a more personal level than seems appropriate when teaching his own discipline. The counselor may want to work in a theme-centered group and may look forward to approaching potential student clientele in a preventive rather than a crisis-oriented way. Both faculty and counselors may want to expand their sense of belonging to the college by teaching Seminar, by breaking out of their department or office a few times a week for this new experience. Almost certainly, Seminar instructors who choose this kind of teaching experience are acting upon an interest in students as learners in a general sense, veering away from their professional interest in students as, say, potential biologists. It is entirely appropriate for early staff sessions to work on getting the instructors to express what *they* want to get out of teaching Freshman Seminar. This not only serves as an analogue to the validating of students' needs, but it also says, in effect, that you, the instructors, are not teaching Seminar solely because you want to give. It is all right, indeed, it is necessary to bring expectations and needs to a helping task.

Summary

Since Seminar instruction requires a combination of teaching and counseling skills, staff development must take into account the previous training of instructors. The academic may need help in eliciting the feelings of Seminar students, and the counselor may need training in bringing more structure into his classroom presentations. The academic who regards himself as a specialist may have trouble with his necessarily generalist role as instructor of Seminar, and the counselor may feel uncomfortable with the formal authority he has as a Seminar teacher who must test and grade his students.

There is a clear advantage in having a Seminar staff composed of both counselors and academics. Their individual areas of interest can often be profitably used in the classroom and, further, shared with the staff group for adaptation in other instructors' classes. The individual contributions of Seminar instructors to the curriculum of Seminar are lost if communication among instructors is not fostered by the coordinator.

In addition to sharing experiences and formats in staff meetings, instructors should be encouraged to write up their class sessions for distribution to other instructors through a materials center. A bulletin board for Seminar staff materials and notices can also reinforce communications among staff members.

Instructors' involvement in students' personal problems can become an issue in staff meetings. Although this involvement poses few problems for the counselor/instructor, the faculty instructor does need information and training on how and where to refer students who have personal problems he feels ill equipped to handle.

Seminar instructors should be helped to be in touch with their own attitudes toward the college and its various policies, for strong negative attitudes can get in the way of straightforward Seminar teaching. If an instructor presents himself as an advocate or adversary of the college, he is likely to reinforce students' preconceived attitudes and thus to prevent them from thinking through their own positions.

Instructors unfamiliar with the college's procedures, policies, and programs will require informational sessions in staff meetings. They can more readily absorb information about *sources* of information than massive doses of factual material. Guests from various service areas of the college can profitably be invited to appear at Seminar staff meetings.

A successful Seminar program will in time become known throughout the college, and requests for guest appearances in the Seminar classes themselves may come fast and thick. The coordinator and his staff must be selective in granting these requests, lest Seminar become a series of guest lectures, and thus hinder the development of student/student and student/instructor relationships.

Group planning in Seminar staff meetings can help to level out the extreme ups and downs of instructors' time commitments throughout the semester. Spreading assignments throughout the semester and not heavily weighing the final examination can help in this leveling-off process.

The coordinator should help his staff acknowledge their own expectations and needs as teachers of Seminar. This is not only similar to the validation of student needs that is attempted in the Seminar classroom; it also helps instructors to get in touch with the sources of their own successes and failures as Seminar teachers.

6
Seminar Sessions: Format

In this chapter we have collected several Seminar session formats, which cover broadly the content range and variety of teaching methods presented in chapters 3 and 4. These outlines of class sessions are intended to suggest rather than to prescribe useful structures for helping students through their first college semester. They have been tried and tested by Hunter College Freshman Seminar instructors: it remains for them to be adapted to the needs of other students at other colleges.

I. Setting the Semester's Syllabus: Cooperative Scheduling

The cooperative approach to planning the semester's syllabus elicits the participation of Seminar students from the first session of Seminar. It is time-consuming but worth the effort, for it involves students in a way that models their participation for the rest of the semester.

Materials

1. mimeographed sheets with a list of topics including topics agreed upon by Seminar staff together with

topics of special interest to the individual instructor
2. mimeographed sheets listing only dates of Seminar sessions for the entire semester

Instructions

After handing out both sheets to each student, ask the group to read through the topics. Wait a few minutes, then ask students to add any other topics they wish to consider in Seminar, and to cross out any topic they consider unnecessary.

Divide the class into pairs, and announce that each pair is to try to agree upon a *schedule* of topics for the semester. Before the paired discussions, a few minutes of large group discussion can be held to elicit the kinds of reasoning that might go into their choice of scheduling a particular topic for a particular time during the semester.

While the pairs are at work, put the list of topics in one place on the board; put the seminar dates on the board in another place. Give ten minutes of paired discussions before reconvening the total group.

The Total Group Discussion

First, ask for any topics not on the printed list, and add them to the list on the board. Some suggestions will be expansions of listed topics; integrate these with those already on the list. "Study skills," for example, may remind a student of problems of privacy at home. This suggestion can then be added to the topic of study skills.

Next, ask students which topics they would like eliminated from the list. It is the rare student who makes a suggestion at this point, but the instructor can remind the group that any topic covered in other classes need not be dealt with in Seminar; "use of the library" may be one such topic.

Finally, go through the Semester's calendar week by week. What does each pair of students have down for next week's topic? Note-taking? Grading systems? Why did they pick these particular topics for these particular weeks? Try to uncover the principle of timely readiness for each topic. Although there will be some minor disagreement over the scheduling of the topics, the syllabus can usually be negotiated so that it is acceptable to the large majority of the Seminar members. Skills topics are usually scheduled early on in the semester, with a scattering of informational topics through the semester. Widespread differences usually indicate that a few students have a specific need that can be dealt with outside of class.

Wrap-up

Once this syllabus is on the board, announce next week's topic and let the class know that the syllabus they have selected will be handed out to them next week. They should be reminded, however, that if special topics of pressing interest or need come up during the semester, the syllabus will be changed to accommodate them.

II. Note-Taking: Getting What's Important down on Paper

Since taking notes from a lecturer is new to most entering college students, Seminar students are likely to feel the need for this session early on in the semester. They understand that taking notes is expected, but the impersonal setting with someone speaking virtually nonstop is likely to throw them. This session is intended to elicit discussion on the reasons for taking notes, to highlight a few note-taking strategies, and to give students some beginning practices on this skill.

Materials

1. a package of carbon paper
2. a written piece that can be delivered as a 10-15-minute mini-lecture

Instructions

At the session previous to this one, ask students to bring in some notes they have taken from classes in high school or at the college. Begin this session by asking students to exchange their notebooks and to look over their neighbor's notes for a few minutes. Ask for comments on styles and formats; list varieties on the board, e.g., full sentence notes, formal outlines, shorthand or other abbreviating styles, seemingly chaotic scribbles and arrows. Stress that note-taking styles are individual; it is whether notes "work" that matters.

The group can then go on to consider what *are* the intended uses of notes. Some students may volunteer that note-taking keeps them alert in class, an interesting by-product of the process. The crucial use, of course, is whether notes help students to review for assigned exams and papers. How do students know when their notes are "good?" The discussion works around to an answer: when they contain material that the instructor considers important enough to include in an examination. How do we know what's important? What cues does the lecturer give? At this point, students volunteer a list of lecturer cues, which may include:

- Lecturer says "this is important"
- Lecturer puts material on the board
- Lecturer raises his voice
- Lecturer repeats material
- Lecturer pauses (implying "get this down")

Mini-Lecture Exercise

Pass out the sheets of carbon paper. Ask students to place the carbon between two sheets of paper. Tell them you will give a short lecture and that they are to take notes, paying attention to the "importance cues" listed on the board. The mini-lecture should come from material of an introductory nature, rich in general interest, e.g., anthropological material on family types. The instructor should use nonverbal and vocal cues, adding intentional distractions such as a questionably relevant anecdote or speaking with his back to the class.

Once the mini-lecture is finished, ask students to trade the carbon copies of the notes they have just taken. Give them a few minutes to compare their own notes with the carbon of their neighbor's notes.

Closing Discussion

The ensuing discussion should focus on the similarities and discrepancies students found in comparing notes. Why did one student consider something important that another did not? What in the lecturer's style was distracting? What can students do about these distractions? Again, put student contributions on the board. These may include:

- Sit in the front row of the lecture hall
- Avoid sitting with other students who may distract you
- Compare notes occasionally with other students to check on the accuracy of your own
- Ask the lecturer to check on the accuracy of your notes

Ask students to practice, during the following week, taking notes with the "importance cues" in mind and to try out one behavior that they feel distracts them from attending to the lecturer.

III. Getting Acquainted: A Memory Exercise

This class format serves two purposes: to help get members of the class acquainted with one another, and to illustrate a central point about the particular learning tool, memory.

Instructions

Ask students to announce their names to the group. Tell them that after all introductions have been made, they will be asked to remember as many names as possible. After the first round of introductions, ask students to write down the names they remember; take a tally of the number of names each student remembers. Then take a few minutes out for announcements not relating to the exercise. Again, ask students to list on a second sheet of paper the names they remember; again, tally the number from each student. Then ask students to introduce themselves once again, adding a piece of information about themselves. For a third time, students are asked to list the names of students they remember, and again the instructor makes a tally. Again, some announcements, and for the final time, students make a fresh list of students' names. Compute the average number of names remembered for each trial and the range at each trial. Put the results on the board:

	Average	*Range*
Trial 1: Names Remembered after Names Only	________	________
Trial 2: Time Lapse	________	________
Trial 3: Names Remembered after Information Added	________	________
Trial 4: Time Lapse	________	________

Discussion Questions

Ask students to compare the average. What was the trend between trials one and two, and between trials three and four? What effect did adding connecting information to another item of information have on the students' recall? How does the exercise relate to experiences students have had in remembering material for exams? What does it imply for the ways in which students might better remember material? Make a list of suggestions on the board. These might include:

- Go over material frequently
- Connect items of information with other information
- Go over material right before you need to recall it (arguable)

Comment

Although this exercise is quite rigid and authoritarian, students are likely to break its formality by joking about their own and others' mistakes. The process is at once simple, challenging, and competitive. The results are a dramatic illustration of the point to be made, and the by-product is that students *do* learn the names of others in the class. (The instructor, alas, may be too involved in running the show to learn as many names as his students do.)

IV. Help, I Can't Find My Way: A Game for Understanding Helplessness

This is a classroom game that can be played early in the semester, when students are in the quandary of not knowing what it is they *need* to know. They may already understand that no one is going to take them by the hand; what they do *not* know is how to take the search for help into their *own* hands.

Instructions

Chairs in the classroom must be movable. Have the students move all chairs to the perimeter of the room. Pick three pairs of students to be primary participants in the game. One member of each pair is asked to stand at one end of the room; the remaining three are to stand at the opposite end. The three students at one end of the room are then blindfolded.

Announce that this is an exercise in getting help. The blindfolded students' task is to move from their end of the room to the other end without bumping into any of the obstacles that will soon be put in their way. They may ask for directions by addressing questions to their helping partners at the other end of the room, but they may only ask questions that can be answered "yes" or "no."

Tell the helping partners that they may not begin giving directions; they may only *respond* to questions, and with only a "yes" or a "no." Now ask the rest of the class to construct obstacles between the blindfolded and helping partners; they can use chairs, piles of books, and even themselves as obstacles. Then announce that you will act as referee, stopping the game when rules are violated and calling stops and starts as the game proceeds.

The Game Begins

Ask only one blindfolded student to begin asking questions. After that student has had a chance to move a few steps, ask the second blindfolded student to begin questions. Do the same with the third. With only one helpee working at a time, the observers and other helpees have a chance to learn questioning techniques from one another.

What Happens during Play

With three students trying to get help, a variety of individual help-seeking styles emerges. One student may insist on moving without asking for directions; his literal blind faith in himself usually ends in disaster, i.e., he runs smack into an obstacle. Other students may show varying degrees of sophistication in asking questions. "Can I move forward?" obviously gives the help-seeker less information than "Can I move forward three small steps?" Some students form their questions better as they go along, by listening to the questions of others or by correcting approaches that get them into trouble. Some may lose their composure when they run into an obstacle, thus getting worse at completing the task. The snickers and laughter of the observers naturally make the task more stressful and embarrassing.

The helping partners' roles are so defined that one helper cannot be appreciably more helpful than another—unless they break role entirely, at which point the referee reminds them of their restrictions. Once one of the blindfolded students reaches his helping partner, the game ends.

Processing the Exercise

Begin discussion of the exercise by asking the blindfolded students how they felt about what they had to do. Responses will come thick and fast: "so frustrated I wanted to scream!," "helpless," "angry, really angry," "foolish." Ask whether or how they changed strategies as they went along. And if they could do it over again, what would they do differently?

The observers are usually by this time eager to comment on what they saw. They may come down hard on the participants; ask them how they might have felt in the same situation. The helping partners, unlike the observers, are more likely to empathize with those they are helping and may express their frustration at the limitations put upon them.

What, your students may ask at this point, does this exercise have to do with being a college student? Ask if anybody has ever been in an analogous situation, figuratively blind and having to rely upon himself to find directions. Some students will easily relate the exercise to experiences with instructors and unhelpful secretaries who seem to force them to ask *all* the questions. Other students may be able to relate the exercise to noncollege experiences of being lost, frustrated, and called upon to get their own bearings by actively seeking help. The instructor can summarize these experiences, explicitly pointing out that in the college setting, in order to *get* help, one must *seek* it, actively and usually persistently.

V. The Rationale for Course Requirements: A Simulation

When course requirements are about to be presented in Seminar, it is wise to precede the presentation with a session that aims to clarify the reasons underlying course requirements. For some instructors, this may be an appropriate time to discuss the history of higher education, with a focus on the evolution of degree requirements at this particular institution. The aim of the simulation exercise offered here, however, is to dramatize the human forces operating to create degree requirements.

Instructions

Explain that a hypothetical new college is planning to admit its first freshman class. A group of seven is to decide what, if any, course requirements students at "New College" are to fulfill before they are awarded a degree. Seven volunteers are to play the Requirements Committee; one is designated the chairperson. The rest of the class is asked to take notes on the committee's deliberations. The committee is then seated in a circle in the center of the room, observers all around them.

The Requirements Committee's Interactions

The members may at first divide into two camps: those wanting some requirements and those wanting none. If the group members do not give reasons for their stance, you can intervene and prod for reasons. If a stalemate develops at this point, those who favor no requirements can be "given a grant to start their own college" and will then be replaced by new members from the rest of the class. Consensus in the reconstituted committee may be reached on a few requirements: English, math, speech. Members may disagree on other subjects of special interest to each of them. A bilingual member may insist that foreign language is a necessity. Someone interested in children may insist that "as prospective parents, we should all be required to take a course in child development." You can then ask the group to settle these differences, giving them a time limit. There may be some horse-trading at this point, which may result in *both* foreign language and child development becoming degree requirements. Halt the discussion when the group seems to have made all the decisions it can make.

Total Group Discussion and Process

Ask what the observers noted down as reasons for requiring courses. Make a list of these reasons on the board. They may include:

- You've got to be well rounded to be "educated"
- You need a broad range of introductory courses in order to make a decision about your major
- You need some knowledge of __________ to get along in the world
- A degree at New College will be regarded as worthless unless there are requirements

Discuss each of these propositions. Ask the group what noneducational forces were at work on the committee. If the committee engaged in horse-trading, does that mean that educational decisions can be made in part on political bases? Point out that although college requirements may be based largely on views of what makes an educated person, some requirements may come about as a result of disagreements among members of the decision-making group. Students may then voice concern that such requirements are not based on reason alone, that they are "not fair." The point can then be made that, indeed, requirements are decided upon by people, not by institutions, and that people make decisions for others on the basis of reasons that others may or may not find valid.

VI. What's in a Grade? A Session on Grading

Grades plague students whether they are adept at getting good ones or not. Achievers and nonachievers alike are concerned about grades. Whatever the merits of different kinds of grading systems, what underlies students' concerns is vulnerability in the face of being judged. In this session on grading, we want to help students acknowledge that having one's work judged can be painful, but that they can be more in control if they find out *by what criteria* their work is judged. This session is most appropriately scheduled *after* students have received grades on their first round of academic assignments, usually four to five weeks into the semester.

Instructions

Ask students to take out a sheet of paper and number from one through four on the page, leaving a few lines between each number. Ask them to write "A grade is . . ." after each number. They are to complete the sentence four times in four different ways. No more than five minutes need be alotted for this.

Reporting Out

Ask students to report their "definitions." Write them all on the board, even if many are similar. Once all definitions are on the board, ask students to collapse the completions into categories. These are all ways of looking at grades; which ones are similar? The following major categories are likely to emerge:

- How being graded makes me *feel* (e.g., "A grade can make me feel elated or depressed.")
- What, literally, grades *are* (e.g., "A grade is an A, B, C, D, or F.")
- What grades are measurements *of* (e.g., "A grade is how well I know the subject.")
- What grades are used *for* (e.g., "A grade is what will get me into graduate school.")

Total Group Discussion

Begin with the consideration of grades as powerful causes of feelings. Why do they have so much power? Then move to a discussion of what really is being measured by a grade. Students may at this point launch an attack on teachers whose examinations did not fairly measure their knowledge of a subject, or say that the measurement was made when the student had "a bad day." Acknowledge that grades are the result of how a *person* performs a task set by another *person,* and, as such, grades are fallible indicators of what one "knows." Over time, however, the cumulative judgments of one's academic performances yield a statistic, the grade point average, which can have a decisive effect on one's future. How, with all this imprecision, can a student feel less helpless as judgments are made of his work?

Ask students whether they know by what criteria their work is judged. Most students will say they do not know, that they have not "been told." Make it clear that it is their right to know. If their English has been judged substandard, then they must know what elements of standard English their instructor is looking for in their papers: proper syntax, grammar, spelling, etc. A little probing will reveal that some students *have* been told the criteria by which their work is judged. In some subjects, however, academicians may be so steeped in their own disciplines that they assume their students understand what is good work and what is not.

Students Set Criteria

To give students some notion of how difficult it is to establish grading criteria and to assign a grade, ask them to trade their sentence completion sheets with another. They are to read over their neighbor's list, assign a grade to that list, and pass the paper back to its owner. In pairs, students are then asked to discuss what criteria they used in grading their neighbor's paper. Then the total class group shares the various criteria used. Put on the board a list of these criteria. You will probably get such terms as *completeness, variety,* and *creativity.* Try to get the students to explain these terms operationally. For example, if Bob was given an A on the criterion of creativity, how would you judge your own paper on that basis? What makes his paper more or less creative than your own?

Assignment

Ask each student to ask an instructor to explain the criteria that will be used in grading an upcoming assignment. Each student is to write a narrative of the meeting he had with the instructor.

VII. Participation in Class

Divide the class into groups of three. Ask each group to share two true stories apiece. One is to be "the best thing that ever happened to me in class was . . ."; the other, "the worst thing that ever happened to me in a class was . . . ." The experience can be from kindergarten on up, but it must be a school experience in the classroom.

Discussion

After fifteen minutes at most, ask that one member of each group be chosen to tell his "best thing" story, another his "worst thing" story. Jot down notes on the board. This part of the session is generally quite lively; the stories—hilarious, frightening, or a mixture of both—will raise much comment from the Seminar members.

A common theme emerges from these stories, and your students can be prodded to come up with that theme. Approval is gratifying, disapproval saddening, or worse, terrifying. From whom does the approval or disapproval come? A student may recount an experience in which praise from a teacher embarrassed him because he felt disapproval from his peers. More commonly, both the adult and peer authorities are felt to be in league against a student who has made some mistake publicly. In either case, the classroom is felt to be an arena where there is great potential for personal discomfort. Ask what students *do* to *reduce* their discomfort. Make a list on the board. It may include:

- sit in the back of the room
- appear to be busy taking notes, shuffling papers, tying shoes
- be the first to talk
- ask a lot of questions
- don't come to class

Point out that although some of these tactics may indeed reduce one's anxiety in class, they hardly help one learn better. What positive, productive things can a student do to make participating in class somewhat easier? Is it possible to lessen the risk of being wrong and thus feeling foolish? Ask the class to consider some classes they were more active in. What was different about those classes? You are likely to get two kinds of responses; students report being more active in a class where they trusted the teacher's good feeling toward them and in a class where they were friendly with other students in the class. How, then, can a student create the conditions for making participation easier? By having allies in the classroom. By meeting the instructor during his office hours. By getting to know one's classmates.

Assignment

Ask each student to pick one class he is now attending, a class in which he would like to participate but has not yet done so. The assignment is that each student must speak up in that class during the ensuing week. The experience will be shared at the next Seminar session.

Further Points of Discussion

Ask students whether they prefer to be called on or to volunteer their participation in a class. You will have students of both preferences. Ask the "forced speakers" to explain their preference and the "volunteer speakers" to explain theirs. Each preference group will tend to explain in terms of lessening the risk to themselves. The "volunteer" cannot bear the risk of waiting to be asked a question he has no control over; he sees volunteering a comment or an answer as a way of "getting participation over with, on some of my own terms." Those who prefer being called on explain that since they did not presume to know an answer, they will not be viewed as being responsible for giving the *wrong* answer. They are more comfortable putting the whole process out of their control.

This kind of division can raise many of the crucial issues to be considered in helping students develop strategies for speaking up in class.

Students who report that they never participate in classes and who are not helped by a session or two in Seminar should be referred to individual counseling. Or a group workshop can be arranged for students who have chronic difficulty in this area. Behavior modification using systematic desensitization has been used with some success for people who fear speaking before groups.[14]

VIII. Where Does the Time Go?

The new college student is often quite casual about time; he sees it as an unlimited commodity. Scheduled classes and deadlines for assignments may foster a feeling that time uses *him,* that he has little choice about using time. This feeling is manifested in such questions as "how much time should I spend on an assignment," or "when will I be able to graduate?" The transition from high school to college brings with it more freedom to spend time as one chooses to spend it; there are no study halls, scheduled mealtimes or bedtimes. It is not surprising, therefore, that time management is for many freshman a very new problem.

The time management session should be presented well enough into the semester so that students have already begun to feel the time pressures mounting. For students in residential colleges, this may come later than for commuting students, who often undertake college with little or no change in their nonacademic commitments; they may still work on weekends or evenings. For all kinds of freshmen, the fewer scheduled class hours than in high school give them the illusion that being a college student requires *less* time than being a high school student.

Instructions

At the end of one class session, hand out a "time sheet" to each student. The time sheet is simply a grid with a square space for each hour in the week. Ask students to keep a record of how they spend each hour in the next week; they are to begin their record immediately after this class session. How detailed is the record to be? Give examples: watched TV, attended math class, studied, traveled home, washed dishes, did laundry. Suggest that everyone fill out the sheets daily. No hour is to be unaccounted for. The completed sheets are to be brought in the next class session and will be used to help them assess how they use their time. No one will be graded on their use of time.

At the beginning of the next class session, ask a few students to put just one day of their time sheet on the board. From these entries, ask students to develop various categories of time use, adding items from their own records as they go. The categories will include:

- home responsibilities
- employment
- classes
- study time
- relaxing alone
- social time with others
- extracurricular obligations
- eating
- sleeping/napping

Ask the students to tally up the number of hours each of them spent in each category, then to list the categories in order of amount of time spent.

Discussion Questions

What were some of the surprises revealed by this data? Are you spending much less time being a student than being a son or a daughter, or an employed worker? Figure out the ratio between class time and study time. Who has the highest ratio? Who the lowest? Ask each of these students to talk about their extreme positions in relation to how they spend the balance of their time. Who in the class would like to spend his time differently? Is that possible, given that student's other commitments? Or is some time use negotiable? How might you negotiate some time spent on home responsibilities? A role-play between student and parents might be appropriate at this point. What areas of time use can you rearrange with yourself? At what times during the week can you do this?

The discussion here can be a rich sharing of personal experiences. The instructor attempts to make distinctions between time commitments that are fixed and those that are changeable. In so doing, he must rely on the feelings his students express. Some will view home responsibilities as nonnegotiable, and indeed they may be; others may see this as an area of time use they can change. The point is to try getting each student to identify some time usage, however minimal, that he wants to change and sees some possibility of changing.

Assignment

Hand out another blank time sheet to each student. Ask students to record how they use their time for one more week. At the top of the sheet, students are to write at least one time-use change they want to make during the next week, e.g., less TV, more study; less time alone, more social time; more study, less home responsibility. Announce that the results of their attempts will be discussed at the beginning of the next class session.

IX. Planning for Next Semester: A Sequence of Seminar Sessions

At a college where students register during one semester for the following semester, Freshman Seminar has a valuable task to perform. The Seminar group can be taken step-by-step through a decision-making process that results in students' being registered and scheduled for their next semester's classes. These sessions should be offered in the few weeks preceding the actual registration. Even in colleges that do not run a pre-registration, the sessions described here can be useful, though they will naturally lack the urgency that comes from planning for an impending registration period.

First Session

What do students want to know before they sign up for a course? Elicit contributions from the class, and put them up on the board. They may include:

- Who teaches the course?
- What is it about?
- When is it offered?
- How difficult is it?
- What are the requirements for it?
- What are the pre-requisites for it?
- What is the course format?
- Does it fulfill course requirements for the degree?

Where can you find the answers to these questions? From written sources, surely, for some of the answers: the catalog, the schedule of classes, departmental brochures. And from other students who have taken the course, some of whom may be in the Seminar classroom. Information gathering can begin by students in the class providing information to one another. Hand out course information sheets (see Appendix B) to each student. Ask students to fill out one sheet for each course they are currently taking and to bring the completed sheets back to the next session of the class.

Second Session

Bring to class a number of signs with general subject areas written on them: social sciences, foreign languages, humanities, etc. Tape these signs up around the room. Ask students to tape up their course information sheets under the appropriate signs. Then they are to take ten to fifteen minutes wandering around this "information gallery," reading the sheets, and noting down courses of interest to them.

The information presented will generate much discussion and questioning. Encourage students to evaluate the information that they have read by querying the students who provided the information. There may be disagreements about the content of a course or the effectiveness of its teacher. Some students will praise self-paced learning formats; others will damn them as impersonal and limiting. The instructor can point out that students are expressing their preferences according to their own learning styles, capacities, and interests. What may be interesting for one may be boring for another, what may be hard for one may be easy for another. Stress that students make appropriate choices (1) on the basis of accurate information and (2) by assessing their own needs *as learners*.

Third Session

Divide the class into pairs, and ask them to share their course choices with each other. They are told to comment and ask questions about each other's choices. In effect, they will be doing peer counseling. A mimeographed form can be provided to help them in this task (see Appendix C). The partners may reveal to each other new criteria for choosing. For example, a student might say "Okay, you're interested in all these social science courses, but hadn't you better start your foreign language requirement?" Or "You've chosen a lot of heavy reading courses; if I were you, I'd replace at least one with a lighter one like Art or Music." The peer counseling session offers each partner the objectivity of the other.

After ten to fifteen minutes of the paired discussions, the entire group meets. Was anyone's mind changed by his partner's comments? Were some pieces of factual information missing? What criteria caused someone to change his mind? Put a list of these criteria up on the board.

The next step, after these sessions on gathering and assessing information, is for students to schedule their course choices. For the next session, ask students to bring in several alternative schedules for the courses they have chosen and, perhaps, altered in response to new opinions and information heard in this session. Tell the group that scheduling, like choosing courses, should be done with their own needs in mind. Are they still half asleep at nine in the morning? Then it makes sense to schedule classes later in the day. Will they have to rush out of a 2 P.M. class in time to pick up a brother at kindergarten by 3:30? Then it makes sense to assemble a schedule that will not rush them. With some of their particular needs in mind, they are to do the scheduling assignment for next session.

Session Four: Scheduling Simulation

Since not all of the student's choices will be available to him at the times he wants them, he will have to make adjustments, either in his courses or in his scheduling of them. The aim of scheduling practice is to simulate a situation in which a student is "closed out" of one of his choices and forced to consider what to do next. If, for example, he must take English composition and the only available sections leave him a three-hour break between classes *or* force him into an 8 A.M. section, what choice will he make? On what basis? If he has chosen to take psychology to fulfill his social science requirement and all sections are closed, what are his alternatives? What are his preferences? In working this out in Seminar, a "decision-tree" develops, on which the alternatives are placed. The key to a student's maximizing his choices is for him to know which choices he prefers to others.

Students arrive at this session with their tentative schedules. Ask a few students to put their schedules on the board. Quite arbitrarily go up to one schedule and cross out a course: "This course is closed. What's your next move?" "But I really wanted to take psychology," cries the wounded student. "Fine, but this section is closed. What's your next move? Can't somebody help him?" Students rifle through their printed course schedules. There's one other section of psychology open, but it's held at the same time as the student's English course. Is there another section? Yes, but it's at 8 A.M. "No way," says the student. "I'd have to wake up at 6 to get there, and I'd be worthless the rest of the day." Can the student take another psychology course? Not without this introductory course. Then how about another social science course? The student relents, "All right, if I have to, I'll take sociology instead." The class goes back to the printed schedule and finds a section of introductory sociology held at the same hour the closed psychology section is held. The problem is solved. In the process, the student and the rest of the class have become acquainted with a step-by-step approach to making decisions by choosing among limited alternatives.

The simulated "closing out" of selected courses can be repeated until most of the alternatives have been covered.

A Final Note on These Sessions

At most colleges registration remains a painful affair to many students, particularly to freshmen who have less experience at it and often less choice (if they register last). Some registration systems are more humane than others, but most still frustrate students who cannot get what they want at the times they want it. The sequence of Seminar sessions takes a large chunk of Seminar time. But, coming toward the end of the semester, the sessions allow for a recapitulation of much of what Seminar has covered earlier in the semester: gathering information, assessing peer opinions, using information about requirements, considering one's own needs as a student, and acting upon those needs in a purposive way. Moreover, since the decisions made through these sessions have such an immediate result, both the students and the instructor can readily see the practical value of their work.

7
Three Classroom Dialogues

This chapter contains three classroom dialogues: one on the difference between high school and college, one on grading, and one on a "parable" by Franz Kafka. These are not actual dialogues but a composite of what has gone on in Hunter's Freshman Seminar over the years.

The Difference between High School and College

In defining the difference between high school and college, the student becomes aware of what he already perceives: that there are more differences between college and high school than meet the eye. Gradually, as these differences are discussed, he comes to see them more realistically; that is, they are less overwhelming. Perhaps the primary difference is that college gives the student more freedom and self-determination. This is apt to befuddle and confuse him, especially if he came from a strict, regimented high school and if his homelife was characterized by controls and parental decision making in which he was not a participant. The pitfalls lying in wait for a student with such a background are numerous. Most frequently encountered is the student who, suddenly given his freedom, loses his bearings, spends his free time in the cafeteria playing cards, sees the school primarily as a social club that provides him with sexual partners, and comes eventually to view academic requirements as an imposition. Such self-defeating reactions are not uncommon, especially among students with a parochial school background.

The other differences between high school and college stem from the above. The foremost is that college requires more work. Unless the student attended a private school or one of the elite academic public high schools he is apt to be surprised by how much reading he has to do. Obviously, this sudden change should, in fact, not be so sudden; that it is sudden is a sorry truth we must accept and work with. For most students, the first response is to make a genuine attempt to cope with the change. This lasts for a few weeks, usually a month. Then some begin to fall by the wayside. Study habits that have not been developed through years cannot be acquired overnight. A fifty-page reading assignment is intimidating; a chapter of chemistry problems is a labyrinth of insurmountable enigmas. The student's problems pile up. Finally, in desperation and disgust, he throws up his hands and says, "enough." We may admire his candor and triumph over compulsive fears; we can only pity the result. Later in the term, one or two weeks before the final exam, these students begin to straggle into our offices. They are anxious and getting little sleep because they are attempting to cram a term's work into a few weeks. The time to cope with this situation effectively has passed, and there is little that we as teachers or administrators can do. The freshman seminar is the ideal place to lay the groundwork that will enable the student to avoid this debacle.

The first step in this defense is a sharing of concern and anxiety. For most students, the volume of required work is overwhelming. What, then, are the methods to deal with this vast bulk of pages? What are the shortcuts? What may be pared down and eliminated? What is essential? All these are questions that the students in the seminar can address.

Probably foremost among these—this must be established before any other problems can be dealt with meaningfully—is the matter of a schedule and methodology for extended study. At least half of all American high school students manage to negotiate the high school curriculum sucessfully without ever solving this problem. One out of three find it difficult to sit for even an hour with a book. The idea of an entire day devoted to study is unheard-of. The change that must be made is, if one thinks of it, enormous. And the degree to which the change can be made determines, in large measure, the success or failure of the student in college and even in life itself. Most American high school students have never learned to work at anything much. This is a bald, unpleasant truth. They divide all activities into two categories: (1) play—fun; (2) work—suffering. One plays as much as he can, and therefore works as little as he can. To do otherwise is to be a masochist.

As long as this simplistic view of the situation prevails, the student is doomed, if not to failure, then, at the least, to mediocrity. For as long as work is unpleasant, only the masochist will choose work; and work done out of a sense of guilt—and it can not be otherwise with such a *weltanschauung*—will lack creativity and joy. An assignment—any assignment—undertaken as a task will be fulfilled as a task. It will be merely dispensed with, gotten rid of, completed, and filed away. The instructor must, therefore, guard against the tendency to preach about the evils of avoidance and the virtue of compliance. This tack may have initial success, but ultimately it only pushes the student farther along a road that leads nowhere.

The problem, then, lies in the grim view of work, a view that because of clumsy, insensitive, unimaginative teaching, has been instilled in the student in his earlier schooling. An academic background chock-full of "make-work" assignments of meaningless readings in dull textbooks, of copying and recopying passages, of rote memorization has made it clear to the student that work—at least academic work—is unpleasant and stupid. All his experience has "proved" this realization. Is it any wonder, then, that when he views his assignments in college, he feels depressed and overwhelmed? To read thirty pages in a meaningless social studies textbook, written woodenly, with little sense of relevance or imagination, is one thing. There are always the movies or a dance afterward. But to read 150 pages of a history of the Civil War with like expectations? This assignment cannot be read in a few hours; it requires a weekend of unremitting toil. No dance, no movies, only endless, barren pages of silly facts.

Viewed thus, the assignment is indeed overwhelming. It is doubtful that any but the hardiest masochist would relish it. The problem, then, is not so much teaching the student to bear adversity as it is to help him see that there is a point to assignments, that learning has a value beyond merely pleasing the instructor, that one can actually derive pleasure from the experience.

Labor is blossoming or blooming where
The body is not bruised to pleasure soul,
Nor beauty born out of its own despair,
Nor blear-eyed wisdom out of midnight oil.

W.B. Yeats, "Among Schoolchildren"

These maxims, trite though they may seem, cannot be ignored or dismissed with the shallow, blasé comtempt they often elicit.

For some, the college experience is their first extended stay away from home. Discussions about the difficulties of dormitory life, the problems of adjusting to roommates, tolerating noise and chaos, living without mom's home-made cookies—mundane as they may seem—can lead the students to greater insight into their emotional state; this, in turn, will help their academic performance. On small campuses, this function is also carried out by a dormitory counselor (often a senior). A general discussion within the framework of the Seminar often will reveal to the Seminar leader where the trouble spots are. These may then be investigated and followed up outside the confines of the Seminar itself.

Graduation from high school and enrollment in college often have a crucial effect upon the parent-child relationship, and the problems inherent in this change might be explored in Seminar. There are different possibilities in this area, possibilities that depend in kind, for the most part, upon the student's socio-economic class. In institutions whose students are primarily from an upper-class background, the problems of separation are usually not crucial, and whatever difficulties do exist are usually out in the open. At the same time the parents want to pay, and indeed are paying, a considerable sum for their child's independence, they are jealous of it. They often complain that the child does not call home often enough, that he does not write, that, above all, he is not appreciative of what the parents are doing for him. The child protests, usually to little effect, but is also not completely guiltless in the affair. In general he does, to a degree, abuse his freedom and neglect his family ties. In time this is usually corrected, but at first students are awed by, and engrossed in, new worlds—other considerations, parents included, are apt to seem insignificant indeed. In time, too, this is usually redressed—as well as the need to be back on good terms with one's parents if one wants support for graduate or professional school.

The reason these splits and frictions heal so quickly is that they are so open: parents are aware of and voice their gripes; students feel put upon and reply with honest, if a little ungrateful, pique. When the student comes from a different and less affluent class, the splits are more traumatic because they are often veiled by a lack of understanding. That most parents want the best for their children goes without saying; this is as true of the wealthiest as the poorest. But as one moves down the economic ladder, complications enter.

Parents who did not themselves enjoy the privilege of a college education sometimes resent the considerable sacrifice they must make for their children. They may have decided to make the sacrifice, and it may even, in the case of many students who attend relatively low-cost public institutions, be a small one. Yet it can cause repercussions ranging from unrealistic expectations to a constant nagging and refusal to understand why the student requires time away from family chores in order to study. If the student is living at home, the parents may feel that although he is not contributing to the family financially, he should make good this unavowed debt by taking care of smaller children, cooking, running errands and the like. This is especially true for female students. The student must have a strong will to resist these demands, since, in so doing, he or she is made to appear an ingrate. Eventually, the tension and bickering this conflict engenders will affect his academic work. Many students who live at home and commute to urban colleges and universities, especially those whose families live in the ghetto, are plagued by such situations. Very often they fail to finish their degree because of the pressure to find a job that will enable them to live on their own or, at least, make a financial contribution to their family. A discussion of this problem, especially if one surmises that it is likely to be prevalent among Seminar students, may help alleviate the situation somewhat. Tales of suffering may be exchanged, thus providing a wholesome release of frustration and anger plus a genuine understanding of their causes. Then one may offer vocational counseling: suggestions about where and how to find part-time employment that will not take too much time or energy. Sometimes these positions may exist within the school itself, often in the form of work-study programs. If more income is required, outside jobs with suitable hours are often available, especially if the college is located in or near a large city. Students need to be made aware of these opportunities; the Seminar can then become a forum for the exchange of valuable information of an extremely practical nature. Students who are working part-time are usually aware of similar openings, either within their company or in similar companies. They have probably spent much time hunting for work and are usually not adverse to sharing their experiences and the solid, helpful information they have acquired.

All of the above—troubling parent-student relationships, job seeking—are problems the student will inevitably face as he matures. In high school, in most instances, he still enjoyed the privileged position of a child, in some ways mature, in other regards still sheltered by his parents. For him, college will be a transition time, a time when he can grow, comfortably and with the aid of teachers and fellow students, into a mature, balanced, and sophisticated adult. One of the prime factors in this increasing maturity is the exchange of opinion and experience. Because our schools are so large, our courses and teachers so specialized, the human contact, the exchange of experience and insight that traditionally was part of the college experience has largely been lost. If conducted wisely, Freshman Seminar can go a long way toward replacing this loss. We would not be so rash as to maintain that it will completely humanize the college experience for the student, but it can be a concrete and meaningful step in this direction.

Discussion

—*Instructor:* I would like you to think about your old high school. This should not be too hard, since it isn't that far away. I would like you to give me some of the things that were different in your high school from the way things are here.

—*Student:* I loved my high school, we had fun after class. We used to go to a luncheonette and have cokes and cigarettes, and we laughed a lot.

—*Student:* We do not have monitors here. In my school you needed a pass when you wanted to leave.

—*Student:* They had all those guards at the doors, and they were awful.

—*Student:* But I am lonely here. I only know the girl who sits next to me in my math class. All I do is go home after school. I have no one to talk to.
—*Student:* Here everybody runs in a different direction.
—*Student:* I go home after school, and my friends from high school go to different colleges, so we never meet. Some of them work. They are busy. Also, my parents work, and so I go home and do homework.
—*Student:* Me, too, I used to have a lot of good friends. My brother works, and he and his friends talk about their jobs. They turn to me, the kid brother, sometimes, "So you go to college, well, well, what is it like?" They don't want to hear anyway, they continue to talk.
—*Student:* This here isn't really like school. It's too big, and it seems that nothing here has to do with anything else. I get lost all the time. It's not like a complete thing. I don't know how to say it. I used to worry when they had staff meetings in high school. Here I think I'd be glad if I knew they were talking about me.
—*Student:* It's just different departments, like a department store. A collection.
—*Student:* One person giving one course, another giving a different course, and all those different buildings. And three hours in between!
—*Student:* And then you have to carry all your books. My chemistry book is heavy, heavy stuff.
—*Student:* Can you imagine all this in the winter? We do not get lockers, right?
—*Student:* In my school we used to have lockers.
—*Student:* We had a homeroom. I liked that because I knew everybody and the teacher knew you.
—*Instructor:* Can you put a name to what you are feeling here? Sometimes putting a name to your feelings helps a little.
—*Student:* I feel weird.
—*Student:* Alienation?
—*Student:* Is that what alienation means?
—*Instructor:* Right, you feel you are not part of the environment. But alienation is a feeling. It is something you feel. It is not something that is altogether "out there." I know, because I have seen students change over their four-year period at school. In another year you'll feel quite different. You will still march from one department to the other in order to take your courses. Nothing on the outside will have changed, but you will have changed. You

will feel less alienated.
—*Student:* That's hard to believe. Why would I feel different?
—*Instructor:* The question should be worded: "What would make a person feel less alienated?" What would make you feel different?
—*Student:* Like someone said, if we knew there is some connection between one department and another. Maybe then I'd feel different.
—*Student:* Do they actually have meetings about students?
—*Instructor:* The answer is yes. Faculty and counselors are very concerned about students.
—*Student:* I bet they never get to know your name. There are 500 students in my bio lecture, how can they get to know us?!
—*Student:* How do they know if you have done your homework?
—*Instructor:* If the homework is to hand in something, they will check this off next to your name. They'll know all right. If the assignment is to read the next three chapters, then the only way the instructor knows whether you've read the assignment is by the grade on the test. And basically who knows whether you've done your work? You do. And that is the most important person.
—*Student:* All they know is your grade.
—*Instructor:* In some courses your grade is all the instructor has to go on.
—*Student:* So you go to him, you give him your name, he looks next to your name and he says B. Right!
—*Instructor:* Yet, you'll have to take my word for it. By the time you have completed your first year there will be a number of people who will know you by name. How can you get an instructor to know you?
—*Student:* If you could catch him, you could talk to him after class.
—*Student:* All my instructors gave me their office hours. You could go see them.
—*Instructor:* Right. Believe me, many of them like it—they like students to come and see them.
—*Student:* In my old school everybody got to know me. I think I would feel less lost if some of the professors knew me.
—*Student:* My sister is friends with one of her instructors, and they go out for coffee.
—*Student:* Going out for coffee makes you feel more at home.
—*Instructor:* I have an idea. I want all of you to pair off—arbitrarily—you two, and you with Mary, and the three of you at the end. I want you to make a date and go out for coffee sometime

during this coming week. Let's get that feeling of alienation out of our systems.

—*Student:* You mean we should meet in the cafeteria?

—*Student:* I do not like the cafeteria.

—*Instructor:* No. You can meet anywhere you like. I think it would be fun to explore the area. See if you can find other places to sit and talk. The assignment is that you meet at a designated spot and find a nice place where you can sit and talk.

—*Student:* Good. I have seen a couple of good places around. I've seen a snack bar in the area, but I don't want to go in alone.

—*Student:* Me too, I saw a bakery with one table and chairs. I just didn't want to sit there by myself.

—*Instructor:* You can discuss the details later. I want to get back to the topic: how to make you feel more at home here.

—*Student:* I really do not know what you are talking about, I felt uneasy in my high school. I always felt uncomfortable in school.

—*Student:* Me too. I felt awful in my school. That's why I am so disappointed. That's why I thought it might be better here. I was sort of going to make a fresh start.

—*Instructor:* You'd like to make a change, do something different. Have you found some place here which you'd like to recommend to the class?

—*Student:* We talk a lot in my sociology class. I like that. You get to know the students and you get to meet them in the hallway, and generally you get a chance to say a few words.

—*Student:* I like to go back to the same place a lot.

—*Student:* I went to the seventh floor roof.

—*Student:* Roof? I'm afraid of heights.

—*Student:* You do not feel you are sitting out. It's very nice. It's a large terrace, it has flowers and trees.

—*Student:* Where is it?

—*Student:* Seventh floor, you can't miss it, there is a sign when you get out of the elevator.

—*Student:* I've already started to talk to some people there.

—*Instructor:* Talking to others makes for a little less alienation.

—*Student:* I got a job in school, and I really love it. I work at the registrar's office. I stand in back of the large counter and hand out forms to students.

—*Student:* Can anybody get a job in the school?

—*Instructor:* How many students have jobs? I'd like each one of you who have a job to say a few words to the class for next week. I want you to tell us how you went about getting a job.

—*Student:* Could we have someone from career counseling? You talked about having someone come in.
—*Instructor:* Certainly, I will make arrangements to have someone from career counseling come and talk to us. Now let's get back to the problem of feeling at home in this large university.
—*Student:* Are there clubs here?
—*Instructor:* Since you asked, you have just cut out an assignment for yourself. You will go to the student activities office and get us the information. What kind of clubs, how do you join, etc.
—*Student:* I saw a sign that said Student Activities. I went in. They have a nice big office on the ground floor. I met the people who put out the paper, and then the student president said hello to me.
—*Student:* My sister told me about student activities, and I went there to get movie passes.
—*Student:* That's a good idea, isn't it. When you see a sign that interests you, go investigate it.
—*Instructor:* So what makes students feel less alienated? Finding their way around.
—*Student:* I was looking for a place to study, and I found the Quiet Lounge. You can sit and read there.
—*Instructor:* All right, I think we have a number of really good suggestions here. Now I want to talk about another way to feel at home. Knowing the rules makes one feel at home. It's always strange to be in a place where you are not sure what is expected of you. There are two kinds of rules at college. Those rules that are written in the catalog. And another set of rules that are implied.
—*Student:* How's that?
—*Instructor:* For instance, an unstated rule is that in an educational institution, during a test, you do not turn to your neighbor and chat. Or, it is an unstated rule that during a lecture you do not start a poker game, or turn on your portable radio and play music.
—*Student:* But how do you learn unstated rules?
—*Instructor:* Actually, you are pros at picking up unstated rules, because you have done it from childhood on. You observe those around you, and learn instinctively without much fuss what to do in situations. In college, one way to learn about all sorts of rules is to come to the Seminar.
—*Student:* Sometimes I guess you have to ask your professor or your counselor. For instance, I missed a test and had to go to the dean of student's office.

—*Student:* What about the other kind of rules? I know there are rules I am supposed to know. I can't ask because I do not know what to ask.
—*Instructor:* Very good point. When we learn rules from childhood on, they are part of our socialization process. Nobody tells us. We watch our mother and father and later on we watch friends and teachers.
—*Student:* I guess you have to keep your eyes open and watch.
—*Student:* How about a rule like cutting class.
—*Instructor:* You know, that is a good example. Because although it says in the catalog that you can only cut so many classes, it still depends on your teacher and on your grade. You have to know what your specific teacher expects from you. We could almost say that in this instance—cutting class—it's written down and implied.
—*Student:* Our teacher says that as long as we hand in the reports and do all right on the tests, he doesn't care if we come to class.
—*Student:* What about the Seminar?
—*Instructor:* Since most of what you learn you have to learn right here in class, since you cannot look the material up in a text book, I would say that I do expect a pretty decent attendance record. What does that mean?
—*Student:* It means . . .
—*Student:* I do not think that we know what this means, I think we ought to ask you, "What does a pretty good attendance record mean?"
—*Instructor:* Yes, it means no more than three cuts. Now I'd like an example of a written rule that you must know.
—*Student:* I have a good one, I think. Advanced French was too hard for me, so I stopped going to class. I didn't realize you had to do anything else. The secretary in the department explained to me that I could have gotten an F in the course. I didn't know I had to drop it in writing. It was lucky she told me.
—*Student:* Why is that?
—*Instructor:* When you attend a class, you must either attend and produce a grade or drop it formally. This place is too big for you to just go to your teacher and tell him or her that you've withdrawn from the class. This way you are left with a clean slate.
—*Student:* It's funny that you have to apply to go to class and then you have to apply not to go to class.
—*Instructor:* Time's up. Remember the coffee-meet. The other assignment: I want each one of you to bring in one unwritten,

unstated rule from this college. Something like, "How many minutes do you wait for an instructor before you vacate the premises?"
—*Student:* Can you do that? You mean, if an instructor comes late, you can walk out?
—*Student:* I didn't know that!
—*Instructor:* The point is not to know it all, but to be eager and willing to find out.
—*Student:* I don't really know how to look for an unwritten law.
—*Instructor:* You'll have to keep your eyes open. An unwritten law in the subway in the morning rush hours is that under no circumstances must you smile at any stranger whose face literally touches yours in the crowd.
—*Student:* I got one: in college you do not need to explain to the guard at the entrance that you are going out for lunch.
—*Instructor:* So long.

Follow-up Session on the Difference between College and High School

—*Instructor:* In India two figures are used to characterize two different types of attitudes towards life. One is "the way of the kitten," the other is "the way of the monkey." When the kitten cries miaw, its mother comes and takes it by the scruff of the neck and carries it away with her. The monkey, on the other hand, hangs on by itself. As we would say, the monkey baby "hangs in there."
—*Student:* How do monkey babies hang in?
—*Instructor:* The baby rides on its mother's back and hangs on tight. Now why do I tell you this story.
—*Student:* I couldn't get the last session we had out of my mind. I kept thinking how passive we were in high school. I kept remembering how I didn't care when they handed me my program card.
—*Student:* Last week we said that in college it's do it yourself.
—*Student:* I didn't realize that college was going to be different. I mean I knew it was going to be different, but I did not know how.
—*Student:* In high school they push you through. You sort of have to do with what they tell you.
—*Student:* I was thinking about that, too. It hit me how some people do it on their own. What hit me was how come I did not even think of doing it on my own.
—*Instructor:* Do they carry you by the scruff?
—*Student:* We could never do it on our own. Not in my school.

—*Instructor:* Are you sure about that? You say that you could not have done it on your own?
—*Student:* I know I was a kitten. I thought every adult knew what they were doing.
—*Student:* When I registered, I realized that in my high school they did not know what they were doing. I was placed into a remedial course in reading.
—*Student:* You didn't read fast enough, that's not their fault.
—*Student:* But the teacher gave me an 85 in English. I thought I was pretty good.
—*Student:* Me too, I thought I was really good in English. I did good in my school. Here I keep finding out that there are so many things I do not know.
—*Student:* But that is why you are here. Isn't it?
—*Student:* I do not mean that I am not learning new things. But there are things you are expected to know in college—and I do not know them.
—*Instructor:* So what you are saying is that you are not prepared to absorb all the new things college offers, because you do not have a basis.
—*Student:* Yes, I do not know percentages, and conversions and algebra, and that is what I need for my basic chemistry course.
—*Student:* I always thought that my teachers were experts, now I do not know anymore.
—*Student:* They didn't care.
—*Student:* They do not care here either.
—*Instructor:* One of the functions of the Seminar is to find out what we can do as of now. As of this moment, who cares about your education? You care. And if you don't, then you must learn to care, you must learn what you yourself can do about it.
—*Student:* But they should let us know.
—*Instructor:* You must learn to ask.
—*Student:* You have a right to know, it's your education.
—*Student:* But I can not help getting more and more mad at my high school. I feel like telling them. They didn't tell us we needed twelfth-grade math.
—*Instructor:* One of the functions of this course is to make you aware of what you do need. Another function is to teach you all the possible ways to get what you need. As one of you said, it's your education. You cannot sit back and have someone feed you. You are kittens. We will help you to change and become monkeys.
—*Student:* How do we do it?

—*Instructor:* Well, I have said this repeatedly: know who to contact when you need help. Counselors are there to help you. I bet few of you saw a counselor in your high school.
—*Student:* I never saw a counselor.
—*Student:* I did once, he said to forget about college, find a nice job. But I couldn't find a job.
—*Student:* But nobody saw a counselor, and I wouldn't have known what questions to ask. That's what I mean. I had no questions to ask.
—*Instructor:* Asking questions, inquiring, doesn't come from one day to the next. I do not want you to beat your breast and cry about what you did not do. Training to become an independent person can be started at all levels of your development. Children can make decisions.
—*Student:* When I was little, my mother asked me to pick what I wanted to wear for school. She let me pick just what I wanted.
—*Student:* Mine used to make a fuss about what I wanted to wear. She used to say, "Now you can't wear a green sweater with a blue skirt." I didn't understand what she was talking about.
—*Student:* Mine did too. She used to say, "Who wears red with pink." She hated what I wanted to wear.
—*Instructor:* So when you are little, you can learn to make decisions like what flavor ice cream, or who you want to invite over to play. That is how you can begin to learn to make decisions.
—*Student:* My parents always asked me where I wanted to go on Sundays. But then we always did what Dad wanted to do.
—*Student:* So we might not have chosen our courses from nursery school up, but we could learn to make other choices at first. In school instead of giving us a poem, they might have asked us which poets we would like to read.
—*Student:* I try to let my little brother make choices, like what he wants to do after school. Then he says, "I don't know all the things we can do." Then I tell him. Then he chooses one.
—*Student:* That is how you can learn to make choices. You make choices that fit in with your age. By the time you get to high school, you should be able to choose some of your courses.
—*Instructor:* Well said: by the time you come to college, you learn about the options you have. You learn to ask the questions that will help you make your choices.
—*Student:* So if our training had been right—I mean ideal—by the time we came to register here there were choices we could have made without leaning on anyone.

—*Student:* You know what to ask.
—*Instructor:* I'd like to see a show of hands. How many of you read the material we handed to you when you came to register? Few, I see. Why?
—*Student:* Man, they hand you so much stuff. Besides, I didn't understand the half of it.
—*Student:* Me too, I had the same thing happen, and now I know that I have to ask. But I was embarrassed to ask. I was really embarrassed. I thought I was the only one who didn't understand.
—*Student:* That's what we are saying. If you want to hang in there, you have to ask.
—*Instructor:* That's right. The difference between the kitten and the monkey is that you get out there and ask, because you want to survive in college.
—*Student:* Instead of mewing you go to your teacher and ask.
—*Student:* My instructor says he has no time to answer questions.
—*Student:* Yeah, they always run out.
—*Instructor:* Well, so here we are, at the crux of the problem. How does it help you if they run out?
—*Student:* It does not. You have to find ways to get the answer.
—*Student:* My instructor said, "Look in the book." I looked and still did not understand.
—*Student:* My history instructor put me down so bad, I never want to open my mouth again.
—*Instructor:* And that is very helpful to your career, isn't it? Let me explain something right here. Asking questions, getting what you need, does not mean you have to practice karate on your unwilling instructor. It means you have to find other ways. Or maybe you have to find more subtle ways of getting answers to your questions.
—*Student:* In my class we ask all the time. In my math class the professor answers all our questions before we begin with new material.
—*Student:* In my economics course the instructor asks us to come to his office if we need help.
—*Student:* I always manage to find a senior in the cafeteria. I like that.
—*Student:* Me too, I like to hang out there. You meet a lot of nice people. Students like to help.
—*Student:* I saw that a lot of instructors have offices and that even if your instructor isn't there, another one sits at the desk. I ask anybody I can find.

—*Student:* I couldn't find a soul to answer questions. I couldn't do my statistics homework.
—*Instructor:* I have a question for you. If you receive a degree, and you go out to look for a job, and the employer says "I hope you know your statistics," do you answer, "The man who taught me had to make a train after class." Or, "The lady who taught me didn't like us to ask questions?"
—*Student:* I would not tell him that at all, I'd probably go out and have someone tutor me. By then I'd know it.
—*Instructor:* So you would have gone for help. Any suggestions from the class?
—*Student:* He said tutoring.
—*Student:* Sometimes it helps to look at another book.
—*Student:* Ask a classmate.
—*Student:* In chemistry I always find someone to help me.
—*Student:* Same in physics.
—*Instructor:* It turns out we have a whole lot of monkeys in class after all.
—*Student:* So when we talk about monkeys, you really want us to be inventive about seeking help. You want us to try different ways.
—*Student:* But sometimes you do not know where to turn, you feel you are in a desert.
—*Student:* Not in college you don't. There are always so many people around. That's part of the fun. You are never alone.
—*Student:* The cafeteria is always crowded. And the seniors like to talk, they like to show off their experiences. It makes you feel good, you feel you'll be in the same situation sometime—in a couple of years.
—*Student:* Same here. Some of the seniors have told me what courses to take next year, which teacher is good, who to stay away from. If they learned it, so can you.
—*Instructor:* What you have just said is so true. There is a lot of hope. Once you recognize the problem, and I think we have recognized it, there are many things you can do about it. Do not sit back and look helpless, go out and get what you need. Homework: I would like you to study the catalog carefully and jot down every agency it lists that will help you to get information. For instance, here on page three, "If you expect a message, the bulletin board."
—*Student:* Oh, I didn't know you could receive messages here.
—*Student:* Do we have to read the whole catalog?
—*Instructor:* (Silent)
—*Student:* No. Only the beginning. You do not have to list course

descriptions. Only where it says: services, facilities, etc.

Grades

A discussion of grading should include the following subjects:

1. Understanding the grading system of the college and using it to the fullest advantage. In all institutions there are peculiarities inherent in the grading system, special grades such as W (withdrawal), Inc (incomplete), WF (withdrawal while failing), Y (repeat course without punitive grade—often used for remedial courses). Knowing the ins and outs of these peculiarities can be very helpful. A student must know how long he may wait before withdrawing from a course without permanent damage to his record. He must know how many W's he is allowed before the registrar's office will question his actions. He must be aware of the stipulations concerning the completion of courses in which he has taken an incomplete. Sometimes he must make these courses up within a month, sometimes within a year. If he misses the deadline, the incomplete may turn into an F. Thus, knowing the deadlines can be crucial. The implications of the Y (repeat the course without prejudice to one's record) should be made clear. The student must be forced to become aware that this grade has been instituted to give him additional time and that he must therefore redouble his efforts. In such situations, students tend to become lax and to cease striving for improvement.

2. The meaning of a grade. Have the pressures of society made the student more interested in the grade than in the meaning of the poem? Because of the tight job market and the fear of unemployment that hovers over most undergraduates, the current trend is for great concern with GPA. This trend is real and cannot be discounted, but at the same time students must be made to see that school is not just a means to an end. They should be encouraged to take

courses for the sake of enjoyment, to explore, to risk poor grades. The value of teacher recommendations (vs. GPA) when seeking admittance to graduate school should be discussed as well as the deadening results of always playing it safe in course selection. It might be a good idea to cap this section of the discussion with mention of some of the illustrious statesmen, artists, scientists—Churchill, Adlai Stevenson, Einstein, Cézanne—who were poor students.

A discussion of grades can be a springboard to help individuals put things in perspective, evaluate themselves in comparison with their peers and competition, and make intelligent choices about vocational goals. The mood of such discussions should be relaxed, yet tough-minded and realistic. Students should not be allowed to drift; peer pressure should be brought to bear to control this tendency. For example, if a student in the sciences is cruising along doing merely mediocre work, he should be questioned about it.* Two tacks might be attempted. For a while, time should be bided, while it is seen whether peer pressure will increase conscientiousness and improve performance. If it does not, then the reality of the situation should be forced upon the student: he should be made aware of the unlikelihood of being admitted to medical or graduate schools with such grades and the corresponding limitations on his chances for gainful employment. He must be able to question himself and seek an alternative field wherein he possesses greater talent. In such discussions, the instructor should assume—whether he believes it or not—that all students have talent and that one of the purposes of the college experience is to enable the student to find out in what areas that talent lies.

*(Bringing grades up publicly is a touchy business. Whether it can be done depends on the characteristics of the individual students as well as the emotional tone generated by the group as a whole. The instructor's judgment in this matter is crucial. If he is uncertain about the propriety of the venture, he is wise to desist.)

3. A special session should deal with the problem of failure in a course, what this portends, how it should be dealt with. Students should be told whether they must repeat the course they failed (this is not always the case) and they should be made to come to grips with the reason for their failure. Sometimes this reason is a lack of preparation, incorrect or unwise study habits, or a lack of genuine interest in the subject. A discussion of these topics can be helpful to the Seminar group as a whole. It should enable them to avoid some future difficulties and to take stock of their present performance. If conducted with sensitivity, such sessions can have a healing effect. Sharing a sense of frustration and defeat often leads the student to see that he is not alone. The comments of other students are generally kind and well-intentioned, and the general effect of such discussions is to soften the blow of an F. Again, however, one must use discretion. There will be some students who absolutely do not want their failures made public; their wishes must be respected.

Discussion

—*Instructor:* Why do we need grades?
(Moans and groans)
—*Instructor:* Everybody groans about grades. I used to groan, my friends groaned and yet, grading goes on. I remember protests, demands for changes, demonstrations to abolish grading. Yet not much has changed. We look at your high school grades when you come to college, and if you continue your education elsewhere they, too, will request your grades from colleges. The two questions for the day are, "Why grade?" and "What is a grade?"
—*Student:* It shows what you know.
—*Student:* It does not show what you know. I always know more than I can show on a test.
—*Student:* I hate grades. I get nervous when I know I'm being graded. When I get graded, it comes out all wrong.
—*Student:* I worry about grades a lot. I want to go to medical school, and they only take people with top grades. Most of the time I do not care about the subject, just the grade.

—*Student:* Grown-ups always say college should be fun. My instructor says students care about a grade and not about the poem they read. But how can you care about anything when all that counts is your grade?
—*Student:* I wish they'd stop giving grades! It is really like punishment.
—*Student:* They punish you for not doing your homework.
—*Instructor:* Aren't punishment and grading different?
—*Student:* When you do not do your assignment and you flunk the test, they punish you by giving you an F.
—*Student:* They expect something from you.
—*Instructor:* I think that's well said. They expect something from you when you come here. I wish you could say a little more about that.
—*Student:* If you study you get a good grade. So they say. But is it always true?
—*Student:* If you study and they test you on what you have learned?
—*Student:* But they expect you to know what they want you to know. You are supposed to do what they want you to do.
—*Instructor:* "They" being the faculty, teachers, instructors. But isn't that a hard and fast rule? You get tested on what you know. You get tested on what your instructor asked you to study, or what the professor talked about in class?
—*Student:* Not always. Sometimes they surprise you.
—*Instructor:* Well, that maybe, but generally don't you agree that your teachers give you work to do and test you on your knowledge?
—*Student:* And when you do not do your homework, they punish you.
—*Instructor:* How do they punish you, by beating you, screaming at you, forbidding you to watch TV, house arrest, tantrums, which is it?
—*Student:* No, they punish you by giving you an F.
—*Instructor:* So F is punishment.
—*Student:* It's the worst.
—*Instructor:* Is an F just pure punishment, or is it a measure of something?
—*Student:* It's supposed to show what you know.
—*Instructor:* I think if it shows what you know, it's not punishment. It would be punishment if the instructor said, "This guy didn't do his reading. I'll punish him and give him an F." Or does the instructor say, "Although he did not answer the questions

on the test, I will not punish this student, I'll reward him with an A." He might say,"The girl doesn't know beans about anthropology, but she's such a nice girl, I do not want to punish her."

—*Student:* I guess what you mean is that if you do not study here in college, you must not expect a reward.

—*Student:* Nobody makes a gift of a grade, right?

—*Student:* No, I guess what you mean is that you must not look at it as a reward or a punishment, but as a measure of what you know.

—*Student:* But I said it isn't a measure of what you know.

—*Student:* All right, then it is a measure of what you know how to put down on paper.

—*Instructor:* Yes, that's right. Yet, do we not reward excellence with A's, and failures with F's?

—*Student:* We are not supposed to look at it as a reward, but it is one.

—*Student:* You know, I never thought about it, but it is a reward when you get a good grade for knowing your stuff. And more so if you get a good grade if you weren't so sure you knew your stuff.

—*Student:* That's a present.

—*Instructor:* Students love to receive such gifts, don't they? Then you do not hear complaints. But you do hear complaints when you receive a grade you feel was unjust.

—*Student:* That's natural.

—*Instructor:* And all this together makes it so confusing. We view grades as gifts, rewards, punishment, and often treat them as something totally detached from ourselves. As if we did not have anything to do with it.

—*Student:* I never thought about it. If I get an A, a B, or a C, I do not think much about it. But I never deserve an F!

—*Student:* Me too.

—*Student:* I feel punished when it's an F. I shouldn't feel that way, though.

—*Student:* You said before a grade measures something. I guess it measures where you stand in relation to other students in your class.

—*Student:* You measure your knowledge against all other people.

—*Student:* Is that what a bell curve means?

—*Student:* No, the normal curve is made after the instructor has graded the papers, he can see how many people failed, or how many got A's.

—*Instructor:* Your grade indicates how you did in relation to the group. The instructor gives you an indication, he shows how you fit in. At the same time, the instructor wants to see how the class did as a whole, and so he grades on a curve. In both cases, you categorize.

—*Student:* I always have to look at my grade in order to know how I'm doing.

—*Student:* But you are surprised when you get an F, right?

—*Student:* When I get an F, I wish we didn't have grades.

—*Student:* We could really have fun if we didn't have grades.

—*Instructor:* But would you study?

(Silence.)

—*Instructor:* The truth, you know, is no matter what you say, you would never study so hard. But it could be more fun, that is correct. But then, learning something new isn't necessarily fun, nor is it supposed to be fun.

—*Student:* I never study as hard when I am not graded. I would study but only study what would be fun.

—*Student:* In some colleges they do not have grades, especially not the first year, they say it gives you a chance to explore.

—*Student:* But in med school and law school, if you do not have a high average, you can't get in. What do you do about not getting a grade? How could they evaluate your work if they do not grade it?

—*Student:* Recommendations, maybe.

—*Student:* You could have your favorite teacher write you a recommendation.

—*Instructor:* That would be great, and then your competitor will have his favorite teacher write him a recommendation. And your competitor might have a favorite teacher who knows how to write fabulous recommendations. Then you are out in the cold.

—*Student :* I wouldn't like to be graded with a recommendation from a teacher who doesn't like you.

—*Instructor:* That's the point. A grade has fewer emotional overtones. That is, a teacher does not have to like or dislike a student in order to record a grade. So it seems to me that no matter how we twist and turn, the grade is still the one most expedient way to answer a question like, "How did this student do in astronomy?" Answer: "He did B work."

—*Student:* Sometimes grades are unfair.

—*Student:* Sometimes a lot of things are unfair. But after all, I'd rather have a grade when I know my stuff than a recommendation. It's simpler.

—*Student:* So grading has nothing to do with punishment. You

only see it as a punishment when you expect better. It often has nothing to do with whether you studied or not. It's that you wished it were better.
—*Instructor:* Right. So the letter grade doesn't have so much to do with whether a person likes you or not. This grade, for all its worth, is yours if you study. It does, in a limited way, measure what you know. It's like eating creamcakes. You cannot hide it from your scale. You might hope against hope that you did not gain weight, but your scale still registers the extra cakes. And in most instances, your grade reflects whether you studied.
—*Student:* But you always say college is exploring. You do not want to be measured all the time. How can you explore when you are getting graded?!
—*Instructor:* True, grading often takes away the spirit of adventure. That's the truth. But here is where your knowledge of the rules and regulations of college can be very helpful. What about cr/ncr? Meaning credit/no credit?
—*Student:* That is when you do not want to get a grade, but just the credit for having taken the course. I'm taking philosophy, and I am taking it just because I like it, I do not want to get a grade.
—*Student:* That's nice, can you do that with any course? Or maybe you could just withdraw.
—*Student:* I need the credit, I do not want to withdraw. I need the three credits, but I need a high index in order to get into graduate school, so I do not want to have to work like crazy in this philosophy course.
—*Instructor:* All right, let's take the case of Mary Jones. Let's say she is a junior, majoring in. . . .
—*Student:* Geology. What can she do with a geology major?
—*Student:* Maybe she can go into ecology. Maybe she wants to predict the weather . . .
—*Instructor:* All right, Mary Jones has completed all her prerequisites and is about to complete all the requirements for the major. This semester she is taking. . . .
—*Student:* Chemistry, and maybe French.
—*Instructor:* And now she wants to take something like . . .
—*Student:* She wants to take a course in cinema.
—*Student:* She gets free passes, right?
—*Instructor:* How's she doing in cinema?
—*Student:* Not so good, she didn't realize that it would be a lot of work.
—*Instructor:* How's she doing in her other courses?

—*Student:* She's all right in geology, but in her chemistry . . .
—*Instructor:* In other words, she cannot spend too much time on this course, right? What kind of a grade does she need in cinema in order to keep her high average.
—*Student:* She needs at least a B.
—*Student:* She can't make it. She has to ask for credit/no credit.
—*Instructor:* By the way, does it matter whether Mary Jones is a junior or a freshman?
—*Student:* Don't you need a certain number of credits in order to request credit/no credit?
—*Instructor:* Thank you, that is correct. You need eighteen credits in order to apply for credit/no credit.
—*Student:* You cannot take it the first semester, then. Too bad.
—*Student:* Do you have to apply for it?
—*Instructor:* Yes. Just a minute, may I have everybody's attention? Before we say another word, I want everybody to find out how to go about requesting cr/ncr for a course. Not more than one small paragraph. You will hand it in next class. All right, where did we leave Mary? Forty-five credits and she is registered in a course in cinema.
—*Student:* What if she has taken the course and gotten nothing? I mean, what if she did not pass the test?
—*Student:* That's all right, isn't it. I do not think that it matters.
—*Student:* She just didn't get anything.
—*Student:* But she loses the three credits.
—*Student:* Not so bad, maybe she wants to try something else now.
—*Instructor:* Maybe next she wants to folkdance.
—*Student:* That's cool, if she didn't need the credit, she didn't lose anything.
—*Student:* How many of such courses can you take?
—*Instructor:* Good question. Also for next time. Please investigate how many credits of credit and no credit you can present.
—*Student:* Where do I find that out?
—*Instructor:* Oh dear, here we go again! I refuse to answer that question. I expect an answer from you next time.

Kafka Story

Although seminar sessions are task-oriented, the discussion revolving around a particular task can lead anywhere. There is so much to learn besides the technical and mechanical aspects of becoming a student that discussion can branch in all directions. The student comes to college for personal and social reasons, and he has to learn to exist on so many different levels that we always try to explore new ways for him to be a student. It is sometimes difficult to describe in prescribed terms what one wants a student to understand and be aware of. One way of describing this is by presenting the material in story form.

The Kafka story illustrates something about how human beings act. The story generally is a follow-up session of discussion about some aspect of making yourself heard in the intricate bureaucracy we call a university: speaking up in class, standing up for your views, pushing to get something done for yourself. Discussion is apt to get lively when it revolves around material taken from literature. It has the advantage of being impersonal, and at the same time it lends itself to an understanding of others and the self.

"Vor dem Gesetz" ("Before the Law") is particularly intriguing and valuable because it begins to acclimate students to a more subtle way of thinking.[15] Many come expecting the world of college to be made up of a simple set of rights and wrongs, of rewards and punishments. If you do this correctly, you will receive that. If you ask politely, it will be given. This is not always true of colleges nor, of course, of life in general. In this regard, college is perhaps a valuable entrée to the frustrations of adult life. The danger here, however, is that the student, frustrated and rebuffed in his attempts to solve his problems, will throw up his hands. The entire institution will become a sham, the world will be made up of *them* (all those who won't give him what he needs) and *us* (he and a few close friends). Looking at matters in this fashion will tend to lead the student deeper into trouble because, expecting rejection and disappointment even while seeking, he will be angry, inflexible, and self-destructive, often precipitating the very reaction he expected. A story such as "Vor dem Gesetz," when analyzed and discussed, will enable the student to make real what he knows—(1) that he is not alone in his dilemma, that the family of "us's" is considerably larger than he might think—and (2) that the situation, in all of its frustrations and sterility, has an absurd dimension to it. Discussing the frequent absurdities he encounters will go a long way toward enabling him to accept them in the right vein, and this in turn should help make him more sophisticated and flexible. This, of course, is the broader purpose for studying literature and philosophy within the college. But—unfortunate absurdity—as the fruits of the study of these disciplines are more and more cried out for, the disciplines are less and less studied. This Kafka would have understood. Used wisely, discussions within Freshman Seminar can provide, in an unofficial way, a good working book list for students interested in acquiring some worldly wisdom. Given the pragmatic thrust of much present-day education, it may be the only place where they will receive such a list.

Before the Law*

Before the Law stands a doorkeeper on guard. To this doorkeeper there comes a man from the country who begs for admittance to the Law. But the doorkeeper says that he cannot admit the man at the moment. The man, on reflection, asks if he will be allowed, then, to enter later. "It is possible," answers the doorkeeper, "but not at this moment." Since the door leading into the Law stands open as usual and the doorkeeper steps to one side, the man bends down to peer through the entrance. When the doorkeeper sees that, he laughs and says: "If you are so strongly tempted, try to get in without my permission. But note that I am powerful. And I am only the lowest doorkeeper. From hall to hall keepers stand at every door, one more powerful than the other. Even the third of these has an aspect that even I cannot bear to look at." These are difficulties which the man from the country has not expected to

*Reprinted by permission of Schocken Books, Inc., from *The Penal Colony* by Franz Kafka. Copyright © 1928 by Schocken Books, Inc. Copyright renewed © 1975 by Schocken Books, Inc.

meet, the Law, he thinks, should be accessible to every man and at all times, but when he looks more closely at the doorkeeper in his furred robe, with his huge pointed nose and long, thin, Tartar beard, he decided that he had better wait until he gets permission to enter. The doorkeeper gives him a stool and lets him sit down at the side of the door. There he sits waiting for days and years. He makes many attempts to be allowed in and wearies the doorkeeper with his importunity. The doorkeeper often engages him in brief conversation, asking him about his home and about other matters, but the questions are put quite impersonally, as great men put questions, and always conclude with the statement that the man cannot be allowed to enter yet. The man, who has equipped himself with many things for his journey, parts with all he has, however valuable, in the hope of bribing the doorkeeper. The doorkeeper accepts it all, saying, however, as he takes each gift: "I take this only to keep you from feeling that you have left something undone." During all these long years the man watches the doorkeeper almost incessantly. He forgets about the other doorkeepers, and this one seems to him the only barrier between himself and the Law. In the first years he curses his evil fate aloud; later, as he grows old, he only mutters to himself. He grows childish, and since in his prolonged watch he has learned to know even the fleas in the doorkeeper's fur collar, he begs the very fleas to help him and to persuade the doorkeeper to change his mind. Finally his eyes grow dim and he does not know whether the world is really darkening around him or whether his eyes are only deceiving him. But in the darkness he can now perceive a radiance that streams immortally from the door of the Law. Now his life is drawing to a close. Before he dies, all that he has experienced during the whole time of his sojourn condenses in his mind into one question, which he has never yet put to the doorkeeper. He beckons the doorkeeper, since he can no longer raise his stiffening body. The doorkeeper has to bend far down to hear him, for the difference in size between them has increased very much to the man's disadvantage. "What do you want to know now?" asks the doorkeeper, "you are insatiable." "Everyone strives to attain the Law," answers the man, "how does it come about, then, that in all these years no one has come seeking admittance but me?" The doorkeeper perceives that the man is at the end of his strength and that his hearing is failing, so he bellows in his ear: "No one but you could gain admittance through this door, since this door was intended only for you. I am now going to shut it."

Discussion

—*Instructor:* I would like you to comment on this story. Remember, there are no wrong answers, so talk away.
—*Student:* He tried to get in, but the doorkeeper wouldn't let him.
—*Student:* So he is a failure, isn't he?
—*Student:* He does not feel worthy to be let in. Maybe he thinks it's heaven.
—*Student:* Could it be heaven, and he is waiting to be let in?
—*Student:* But he is waiting, just sitting there and waiting. It makes me mad. He should do something about it.
—*Student:* But he thinks he's done something about it: he asked.
—*Student:* He believes he's done something, but he hasn't.
—*Instructor:* Explain.
—*Student:* It's like handing him bricks to make a building. But giving him bricks doesn't make a building.
—*Instructor:* What do you think you need in order to make a building out of a pile of bricks?
—*Student:* Maybe you need a plan, some thought, training. I don't know. Maybe you have to stick to it.
—*Instructor:* Persistence?
—*Student:* Didn't the man think he tried? I mean we think we try, but we fall flat on our faces.
—*Student:* Maybe if we persist. Maybe if we would say, I'm going to go out there and do it.
—*Student:* We are too negative. Don't say I try, say I will do it.
—*Student:* I do not think I could feel that way about it. The guy is sitting in front of that door, waiting. When he gives him some of his possessions, he really thinks he is giving him something in exchange for being let in.
—*Student:* Do you think maybe he gives him something he has accomplished?
—*Student:* No, he wants to please him.
—*Student:* I knew he wasn't going to make it in. And I think he accepts the fact he isn't going to make it. He is defeated from the start.
—*Instructor:* You are saying that the guard says, "You can't get in," and the man says "that's right, I can't." What does the class think of that?
—*Student:* He tries to bribe him.
—*Student:* Bribing is part of the law. I mean it's the other side of the law.
—*Student:* I wish he would say, "to hell with you," and push his

way in.
—*Instructor:* Is that how it works?
—*Student:* They are in the same boat, both men are, they both respect the law. Maybe you do not have to do it that way.
—*Student:* That's what I said, he knows he's not going to make it.
—*Student:* He goes about it wrong, I mean it's the wrong way of trying.
—*Student:* If he had felt sure of himself, he would have gone right in. He feels unfit to go in.
—*Student:* Maybe he could have gone in at first. His rap was too long.
—*Instructor:* Can you elaborate that a little? You say we expect him to get in, but somehow he missed the boat.
—*Instructor:* We expect the doorkeeper to change his mind.
—*Student:* I wonder, is the doorkeeper responsible for keeping him out?
—*Student:* Boy, sometimes I think I have accomplished nothing, but this guy asks the fleas to help him get in.
—*Student:* I think we do this all the time. We are always asking the wrong people for help, or we are asking people for help when actually the only person who can help is ourselves.
—*Student:* We bark up the wrong tree. The fleas can't help.
—*Instructor:* So we are always asking other people to do a job for us. And somewhere we know that the fleas cannot help us.
—*Student:* If you have a problem, you go around in circles instead of solving it, we ask different people for advice.
—*Student:* When I have an exam—sometimes—when the stuff won't go into my head, I call my girlfriend, I make tea, I pray, and I know that the only thing that really helps is to sit and study.
—*Instructor:* Good.
—*Student:* Yeah, but the doorkeeper reminds him that he is only the first doorkeeper, you forget about the other doorkeepers.
—*Student:* I think so, too. I think if only I could solve this problem, I'll never have another one.
—*Student:* I say, if I can get through this difficult period, nothing will ever be so bad, or my life will be changed.
—*Instructor:* Do you think that while he sits out there on the bench, he worries about all the doorkeepers at the same time?
—*Student:* I bet he does, but that is wrong.
—*Student:* I cross that bridge when I come to it.
—*Student:* I think about that tomorrow.
—*Student:* The problem he has is to get in.

—*Student:* But the doorkeeper does say, "No one but you can get in here."
—*Student:* He gives up.
—*Student:* I still state that he is going through life, putting up his own obstacles. He is making up problems for himself.
—*Student:* When he is dying, the doorkeeper tells him the truth.
—*Student:* Why the truth, he never said anything different before!
—*Student:* I wish the guy would get in. Maybe when he dies he gets in.
—*Student:* I do not think he gets in.
—*Student:* He tried to be law-abiding, but he didn't know what the law looked like.
—*Student:* I don't know what the law looks like.
—*Instructor:* The man tries to get in, a man stops him and says, "You can't do that," and so he remains in front of the door.
—*Student:* He got hung up with his own lack of knowledge.
—*Student:* He has to bribe, right? He doesn't know any other way. But he wasted his life sitting and bribing, and neither of these things helped him one bit.
—*Student:* The door will be closed anyway.
—*Student:* That's a terrible story. He found out too late that no one can help him.
—*Student:* He took too much stuff with him. It burdened him.
—*Student:* I guess you can never wait for anybody to say to you, "Not yet, maybe later."
—*Student:* Naw, he should have pushed the guy and jumped.
—*Student:* The man says sit down, and he just sits. He doesn't even question it. He just curses.
—*Instructor:* Good point. Cursing is not questioning.
—*Student:* The doorkeeper says, "If you are good, I'll let you in."
—*Instructor:* Very good. The man doesn't question this either.
—*Student:* It's the damn respect for authority.
—*Student:* Bribery didn't work, but he couldn't think of another way. Isn't it funny that he couldn't think of another way to get in!
—*Student:* Do you think when the author wrote this, he had a very clear-cut meaning in his head?
—*Student:* I think I can answer that. I was writing a poem once, and I asked the poem, "Is there a god?" and the poem answered me.
—*Student:* The poem speaks back to you?
—*Student:* So the poet doesn't know the answer, and when he writes, he comes closer to his answer.
—*Student:* So you have questions inside, and when you write a

paper, sometimes the questions get answered.
—*Instructor:* Sometimes words do not tell what we mean, so we have to put it into a story and show a situation. If he could have put this story into perfect words, we would not be sitting here and guessing as to what he meant. We have about ten minutes left. Do you want to continue?
—*Student:* Sure. He is a compliant personality.
—*Student:* It's like the phrase, "nothing ventured, nothing gained."
—*Student:* He wants to have it all very pleasant. He wants to make sure it all comes out all right. I mean, do we not do that? We want to risk something, but only if someone tells us go ahead, it's all right.
—*Instructor:* What about the opposite? Have any of you been in a situation in school where someone has said to you, "You can't do that."?
—*Student:* It happened to me, and I was amazed that I went ahead and did it anyway. I wanted to take gym this semester and all the sections were closed. So I went to the gym class that would have fit into my schedule and asked the instructor. You know what, he said yes. I got so encouraged, I then went and changed my lab section, although the bio department said it couldn't be done.
—*Instructor:* Great example. She was told all sections were closed, she tried anyway, got it for two of her classes. I think that's pretty good and illustrates much of what we were talking about here.
—*Student:* But aren't there times when "no" means "no."?
—*Student:* You are asking the fleas.
—*Student:* You wouldn't know until you try, though.
—*Student:* And also, there may be another way, even if they say "no." My high school counselor told me to go to a vocational school. But I didn't listen to him, and here I am in college.
—*Student:* It's all so confusing. It's so hard to understand.
—*Instructor:* That's for sure, it is not easy. But I think we have a lot of food for thought here today. I do not want you to bring in a written assignment. I want you to be aware of how you go about getting what you need. Watch and observe yourself. How do you act when a bus is crowded and you have to get to work? When someone says no, do you wait patiently, do you get angry, do you sneak in? Learn how you behave when a secretary tells you you cannot see the chairman. Maybe you are the kind of person who hopes that the following bus will be less crowded. Maybe you hope

that even if you did not study your German verbs for the test you'll manage. Maybe you hope that if you are a good boy, you will be "let into" the bio lab. You are to bring in as many instances of this kind of behavior as you can observe.

Appendix A: Course Description

Title:	Freshman Seminar	98 001	1 hour, 1 credit

Course Description:	Small groups of freshmen; dealing with skills, planning and attitudes required to best utilize the college setting.

I. Rationale

There are elements of learning and decision making not covered in the traditional curricular structure that are essential to the student's educational process. These include the selection of courses, study skills, making long-term educational plans, placing course work in a broader context of student development, dealing with personal difficulties, and adjusting to inadequacies in pre-college preparation. At Hunter, the student must face these issues with added complications caused by varying degrees of preparation among students, crowded conditions that decrease opportunities of faculty-student contact, liberal basic requirements that ask the student to do much of his own planning, uncertainties in what to prepare for due to societal changes, and difficulties in financing an education and dealing with home problems.

To help students at Hunter face these issues in an organized way, a freshman seminar course is proposed. This course will provide an opportunity for freshmen to work with faculty and other students in the consideration of issues designed to assist them in making decisions and in dealing with the many interrelated problems that have a bearing on their academic career.

II. Organization

The course should be open to all freshmen who wish to enroll, but practical matters require an alternative. Therefore, the course should be strongly recommended for all open admission freshmen, who may have a greater need for the course than other freshmen and if room permits, other interested freshmen should be allowed to enroll. Each section will meet for one hour per week for one semester. To emphasize that this is an integral part of the student's educational experience, one credit is to be given for completion of the course, which is to be graded on a credit/no credit basis. The course is to be taught and coordinated by faculty from the Office of Academic Advising and Student Services.

III. Outline: Specific Areas to Be Covered

A. Academic planning
   1. Course selection
   2. Grading system
   3. General requirements
   4. Probation, suspension, dean's list
   5. Balancing schedules

B. Approaches to academic work
   1. Managing time
   2. Note-taking
   3. Exam-taking
   4. Improving study skills
   5. Class participation
   6. Making use of college facilities

C. Long-term goals
    1. Choice of major
    2. Consideration of career possibilities
    3. Identification of personal strengths and weaknesses
    4. Consideration of interests and abilities as they relate to future planning

D. Personal adjustment
    1. Making plans to finance the education
    2. Coordination of part-time job and other financial obligations with academic expectations
    3. Dealing with conflicts regarding family expectations and academic responsibilities
    4. Relating to other students
    5. Participating in nonacademic activities
    6. Dealing with social issues, including health matters and external societal pressures
    7. Where to find assistance
    8. Dealing with daily frustrations, in and out of the classroom

Appendix B

FRESHMAN SEMINAR
Course Information Sheet

Course Number____

Course Title____

Instructor____

1. Description of the course (what material is covered).

2. Format of the course (lecture, discussion, lab, self-paced, etc.).

3. What do you like about the course?

4. What did you dislike about the course?

5. Would you recommend this course to a friend? Why or why not?

Appendix C

Student's Name ____________________

Dr. James Koutrelakos
Instructor

PROGRAM PLANNING EXERCISE

The purpose of this exercise is to help you better understand how to develop a program plan. By evaulating someone else's program, you will be better able to plan your own.

A. Student Program

1. Name of student whose program you are evaluating: ________________

2. This student's Fall and Spring program:

Fall Courses	Cr.	Spring Courses	Cr.

Total Cr. ____

3. If the student is employed, how many hours does he work weekly? ______

4. Home responsibilities (check one): Light __ Moderate __ Heavy __

5. Student strengths and weaknesses:

   a) What kind of courses does the student find most difficult? ______

   b) What kind of courses does the student find easiest? ______

6. Alternate courses: ________________

B. Evaluation of Student Program

1. Is the student correctly following the remedial sequence? Yes __ No __

2. If the student is ready for 17.120, is he planning to take this course? Yes __ No __

3. Is the student taking mostly Basic Prescription Courses? Yes __ No __

4. What is your opinion of the total credit load the student is planning to carry? Too little __ Too much __ Okay __

5. What is your opinion of the student's plan in terms of program balance? Poor __ Fair __ Very good __

6. What is your overall opinion of the student's program? Below average __ Average __ Very good __

Notes

1. Joseph S. Lombardi, "The College Counseling Center and Preventive Mental Health Activities," *Journal of College Student Personnel* 15, no. 6 (1974): 435-438.

2. Leona E. Tyler, *The Work of the Counselor* (New York: Appleton-Century-Crofts, 1961), p. 17.

3. Robert W. White, *Lives in Progress: A Study of the Natural Growth of Personality,* 2d ed. (New York: Holt, Rinehart and Winston, 1966); Graham B. Blaine and Charles C. McArthur, *Emotional Problems of the Student,* 2d ed. (New York: Appleton-Century-Crofts, 1971).

4. John Gardner, personal communication, July 1977.

5. Joshua R. Gerow and R. Douglas Lyng, *How to Succeed in College: A Student Guide Book* (New York: Charles Scribner's Sons, 1975); Cathy Crafts and Brends Hauther, *Surviving the Undergraduate Jungle; A Student's Guide to Good Grades* (New York: Grove Press, 1976).

6. George Weigand and Walter S. Blake, Jr., *A Study Skills Manual: College Orientation* (Englewood Cliffs, N.J.: Prentice-Hall, 1955).

7. Clifford D. Morgan and James Deese, *How to Study,*

2d ed. (New York: McGraw-Hill, 1969); Jacob Millman and Walter Pauk, *How to Take Tests* (New York: McGraw-Hill, 1969).

8. Sidney B. Simon, Leland W. Howe, and Howard Kirschenbaum, *Values Clarification: A Handbook of Practical Strategies for Teachers and Students* (New York: Hart Publishing Co., 1972).

9. Blaine and McArthur, *Emotional Problems of the Student,* especially McArthur's chapter, "Distinguishing Patterns of Student Neuroses," pp. 52-72.

10. *American College Dictionary,* s.v. "seminar."

11. See below, chapter 6, "Setting the Agenda: Cooperative Scheduling."

12. James R. Davis, *Teaching Strategies for the College Classroom* (Boulder, Colo.: Westview Press, 1976), pp. 93-98.

13. J. William Pfeiffer and John E. Jones, *A Handbook of Structured Experiences for Human Relations Training,* vols. 1-6 (Iowa City, Iowa: University Associates Press, 1969—).

14. Gordon L. Paul, *Insight vs. Desensitization in Psychotherapy: An Experiment in Anxiety Reduction* (Stanford, Calif.: Stanford University Press, 1966). See especially his Appendix D.

15. Franz Kafka, *Parables and Paradoxes* (New York: Schocken Books, 1961), pp. 61-65.

Selected Bibliography

Adler, Mortimer J. *How to Read a Book: The Art of Getting a Liberal Education.* 6th paperback ed. New York: Simon and Schuster, 1960. This is a must for students. Professor Adler says, "I have tried to write a light book about heavy reading." Such dry materials as study habits are made interesting.

Casteel, J. Doyle, and Stahl, Robert J. *Value Clarification in the Classroom: A Primer.* Pacific Palisades, Calif.: Good Year Publishing Co., 1975. The individual expression of values may be taught. This book is designed to help the student develop and facilitate behavior associated with value clarification.

Clark, Burton R. *The Problems of American Education.* New York: A New York Times Book, Division of Franklin Watts, 1975. This is an up-to-date history of social conditions as they relate to education and a description of the crisis of purpose and identity in higher education.

Crafts, Cathy, and Hauther, Brends. *Surviving the Undergraduate Jungle: A Student's Guide to Good Grades.* New York: Grove Press, 1976. This is a sophisticated and humorous guide, written by two Columbia University students. It makes good suggestions for the student who needs some "how to" pointers.

Cremin, Lawrence A. *The Transformation of the School: Progressivism in American Education, 1876-1957.* New York: Vintage Books, Caravelle ed., 1964. A history of progressive education that gives an overall picture of the social and psychological aspects that feed into it—and which again raises the question of values, by asking specifically about American education. How can the values of individuals be reconciled with the teaching of groups of students?

Erikson, Erik H. *Identity, Youth and Crisis.* New York: W.W. Norton and Co., 1968. Discussion of the identity problem and its dimensions and meaning for the adolescent and young adult. A collection of essays on subjects through which the young person tries to define his or her identity.

Gelatt, H.B.; Varenhorst, Barbara; Caney, Richard; and Miller, Gordon P. *Decisions and Outcomes.* New York: College Entrance Examination Board, 1973. This is a fine book for young adults. It deals with structured ways to come to intelligent decisions about subjects people face at the beginning of a college career. A leader's guide is attached.

Gerow, Joshua R., and Lyng, R. Douglas. *How to Succeed in College: A Student Guide Book.* New York: Charles Scribner's Sons, 1975. Advice and suggestions for the college freshman. Many of the problems freshmen encounter are universal. Based on experiences of many students.

Graham, Sheila Y. *Harbrace College Workbook—Form A.* New York, Chicago, San Francisco, Atlanta: Harcourt Brace Jovanovich, 1941. This is a strictly utilitarian book. If the instructor wishes to go into grammar in practice sessions, this single workbook gives exercises and definitions.

Hargraves, David H. *Interpersonal Relations and Educa-*

tion. London and Boston: Routledge and Kegan Paul, 1972. Role consists of a set of expectations. "It is because some individuals do not conform to the expectations that we must distinguish role from role performances," says David H. Hargraves. This book studies the self as it arises from social experience of interacting with others. It discusses the role of the student and clarifies the roles teachers play.

Havice, Charles. W., ed. *Campus Values: Some Considerations for Collegians.* New York: Charles Scribner's Sons, 1968. A collection of readings by various authors, this volume is intended to be used "as a springboard for discussion and further reflection" on such issues as the generation gap, drugs, sex, plagiarism, and protest. Nothing here about student skills. An appropriate text for an issues-oriented Freshman Seminar and a population of academically prepared and sophisticated college freshmen.

Henry, Jules. *On Education.* New York: Random House, A Vintage Book, 1966. Describes the conflict between education and culture; education as it affects ethnic groups. Describes the plight of the culturally deprived in school.

Illich, Ivan. *Deschooling Society.* New York: Harper and Row, 1971. This outspoken book about the state of education is a good book for students to read. It is so controversial that it makes an excellent departure point for discussion.

Kirschenbaum, Howard; Simon, Sidney B.; and Napier, Rodney W. *Wad-Ja-Get? The Grading Game in American Education.* New York: Hart Publishing Co., 1971. Grading is a very controversial topic in American education. This book deals with the dehumanizing aspect of grading. Three professors of education discuss the issues surrounding grading, as they are experienced by millions of students and teachers every day. The book is written in the form of a novel.

Lass, Abraham H., and Wilson, Eugene S. *The College Student's Handbook.* New York: David White Co., 1970. This attempt at a comprehensive "how to" succeed in college is addressed to the students of a residential college. The tone seems somewhat condescending, and the treatment of many areas seems cursory. Not recommended.

Marclay, Andrew M.; Crano, William D.; Thornton, Charles; and Werner, Arnold. *How to Do a University.* New York: John Wiley and Sons, 1971. This book maps out what students can expect from college and defines the function of a college or university as a place where students can have the time and the chance to research and study certain subjects that will lead to the student's development as a person. The book is largely concerned about what the student has to contribute to this venture, and it is therefore good material for assignment in the Seminar.

Miles, Mathew B. *Learning to Work in Groups.* New York: Horace Mann Lincoln Institute of School Experimentation, Teachers College, Columbia University, 1967. Although this book is written with groups in mind, it offers suggestions for seminars. It has a great deal of helpful material for training the teacher-counselor. It has a lot of training material with reference to activities.

New York State Personnel and Guidance Association. *Tips to Improve Personal Study Skills.* Albany, N.Y.: Delmar Publishers, 1968. The pamphlet maintains that although teachers advise students on what to study, few take the time to teach "how to." Tips gather a great deal of information on how to study and lists some all students need to know as well as many designed to fit particular student needs.

Pitcher, Robert W., and Blaushild, Babette. *Why College Students Fail.* New York: Funk and Wagnalls, 1970.

This book, using data from over 600 college dropouts, explores the causes of failure in college. Relatively sophisticated, yet written in lay language, it is addressed to parents of college students or prospective college students. The authors discuss many causes of college failure: family, the creative and unmotivated student, and colleges themselves.

Robinson, Francis P. *Effective Study*. 4th ed. New York: Harper and Row, 1970. A study-skills text, this book provides advice based upon documented research, diagnostic tests, and practice exercises for the college student. It may be a bit ponderous for the freshman, but it avoids the faddishness and condescension of some more recent "how to" books. Good for a Freshman Seminar that emphasizes study techniques.

Sterling, Philip, ed. *Interviews with Thirty Inner-City School Teachers in Boston, Cleveland, Detroit, New York, Philadelphia and Washington, D.C.* New York: Random House, A Vintage Book, 1973. This book, which gives thirty interviews with inner-city teachers, presents a variety of thoughts and opinions on social and psychological issues as they relate to education. Since teachers have such an influence on students, their values are of interest.

Szasz, Thomas S. *Ideology and Insanity: Essays on the Psychiatric Dehumanization of Man*. Garden City, N.Y.: Doubleday and Co., Anchor Books, 1970. Essays on a number of aspects of society that show man in conflict between his internal self and the externals that limit society and individuals. There is a discussion about mental health services in the school.

Voeks, Virginia. *On Becoming an Educated Person: An Orientation to College*. Philadelphia: Saunders Co., 1964. Despite the title, which is bound to put many students off, Voeks's book is clear, well-organized, and addressed directly to the college freshman. It includes sections on study techniques as well as sections on the student as a growing person with feelings. Especially good is the chapter entitled "Personality Characteristics Which Handicap Us; Some Ways To Change Them." A valuable, unpretentious, and nonfaddish text.

Waldhorn, Arthur and Hilda. *The Rite of Becoming*. New York and Cleveland: World Publishing Co., 1969. Studies and stories by a collection of authors dealing with phases of growing up. The mixture of literature and psychology makes the collection a good takeoff point for discussions.

Walter, Tim, and Siebert, Al. *How to Be a Better Student and Still Have Time with Your Friends*. New York: Holt, Rinehart and Winston, 1976. This book compiles in readable form many tips on how to study without falling asleep over your books.

Weigand, George, and Blake, Walter S., Jr. *A Study Skills Manual: College Orientation*. Englewood Cliffs, N.J.: Prentice-Hall, 1955. This is an excellent book on study skills. If the instructor is willing to put in a number of class hours on study skills, this may be a good text to recommend.